The Christian Archetype

Marie-Louise von Franz, Honorary Patron

**Studies in Jungian Psychology
by Jungian Analysts**

Daryl Sharp, General Editor

The Christian Archetype

A Jungian Commentary on the Life of Christ

Edward F. Edinger

INNER CITY BOOKS

Canadian Cataloguing in Publication Data

Edinger, Edward F. (Edward Ferdinand), 1922-
  The Christian archetype

(Studies in Jungian psychology by Jungian analysts; 28)

Bibliography: p.

Includes index.

ISBN 0-919123-27-9

1. Jesus Christ—Psychology. 2. Jung, C. G. (Carl
Gustav), 1875-1961. 3. Individuation. I. Title.

BT590.P9E35 1987   232   C87-093416-3

INNER CITY BOOKS
Box 1271, Station Q, Toronto, Canada M4T 2P4
Telephone (416) 927-0355

Honorary Patron: Marie-Louise von Franz.
Publisher and General Editor: Daryl Sharp.
Editorial Board: Fraser Boa, Daryl Sharp, Marion Woodman.
Executive Assistants: Vicki Cowan, Ben Sharp.

INNER CITY BOOKS was founded in 1980 to promote the
understanding and practical application of the work of C.G. Jung.

Index by Daryl Sharp

Printed and bound in Canada by Webcom Limited

Contents

See final page for descriptions of other Inner City Books

Frontispiece. Annunciation. (*Roger van der Weyden*)

What happens in the life of Christ
happens always and everywhere.
In the Christian archetype all lives
of this kind are prefigured.
—C.G. Jung, *Psychology and Religion.*

Illustrations

Preface

This book is an attempt to present in orderly fashion C.G. Jung's interpretation of the Christian myth. He is concerned to rescue for modern man the spiritual treasures which traditional religion can no longer carry. For many, God has abandoned his erstwhile dwelling in the churches and is not likely to return. "We are living in what the Greeks called the *kairos*—the right moment—for a 'metamorphosis of the gods,' of the fundamental principles and symbols."[1] The *numinosum* is seeking a new incarnation. We can expect to find help in understanding this event by examining that great incarnation myth, the life of Christ.

1. Jung, "The Undiscovered Self," *Civilization in Transition*, CW 10, par. 585. [CW refers throughout to *The Collected Works of C.G. Jung*.]

Introduction

The drama of the archetypal life of Christ describes in symbolic images the events in the conscious life—as well as in the life that transcends consciousness—of a man who has been transformed by his higher destiny.[1]

The life of Christ, understood psychologically, represents the vicissitudes of the Self as it undergoes incarnation in an individual ego and of the ego as it participates in that divine drama. In other words the life of Christ represents the process of individuation. This process, when it befalls an individual, may be salvation or calamity. As long as one is contained within a church or religious creed he is spared the dangers of the direct experience. But once one has fallen out of containment in a religious myth he becomes a candidate for individuation. Jung writes,

> In so far as the archetypal content of the Christian drama was able to give satisfying expression to the uneasy and clamorous unconscious of the many, the *consensus omnium* raised this drama to a universally binding truth—not of course by an act of judgment, but by the irrational fact of possession, which is far more effective. Thus Jesus became the tutelary image or amulet against the archetypal powers that threatened to possess everyone. The glad tidings announced: "It has happened, but it will not happen to you inasmuch as you believe in Jesus Christ, the Son of God!" Yet it could and it can and it will happen to everyone in whom the Christian dominant has decayed. For this reason there have always been people who,

1. Jung, "A Psychological Approach to the Trinity," *Psychology and Religion*, CW 11, par. 233.

15

not satisfied with the dominants of conscious life, set forth—
under cover and by devious paths, to their destruction or salvation—to seek direct experience of the eternal roots, and,
following the lure of the restless unconscious psyche, find
themselves in the wilderness where, like Jesus, they come up
against the son of darkness.[2]

Through the centuries a series of images has crystallized
out of the collective psyche to serve the function of "amulet
against the archetypal powers." These nodal points of Christian art and experience express the essential stages in the life
of Christ as chosen by the objective psyche itself, the *consen-
sus omnium*. There is no specific number of these images. I
have chosen fourteen of the most prominent ones—the fourteen chapters of this book—to consider psychologically. This
series of images depicts the unfolding of the Christian myth,
which can be summarized as follows:

God's preexistent, only-begotten Son empties himself of
his divinity and is incarnated as a man through the agency of
the Holy Ghost who impregnates the Virgin Mary. He is born
in humble surroundings accompanied by numinous events and
survives grave initial dangers. When he reaches adulthood he
submits to baptism by John the Baptist and witnesses the descent of the Holy Ghost signifying his vocation. He survives
temptation by the Devil and fulfills his ministry which proclaims a benevolent, loving God. After agonizing uncertainty,
he accepts his destined fate and allows himself to be arrested,
tried, flagellated, mocked and crucified. After three days in
the tomb, according to many witnesses, he is resurrected. For
forty days he walks and talks with his disciples and then
ascends to heaven. Ten days later, at Pentecost, the Holy Ghost
descends, the promised Paraclete.

The sequence of images which constitutes the Christian

2. *Psychology and Alchemy,* CW 12, par. 41.

myth begins and ends with the same image—the descent of
the Holy Ghost. This suggests that the sequence may express
a circular process which might be arranged as follows:

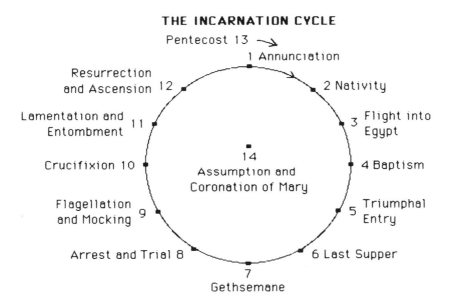

THE INCARNATION CYCLE

Pentecost is a second Annunciation. Just as the first Annunciation is followed by the birth of Christ, so the second Annunciation is followed by the birth of the Church.[3] The Church as
the body of Christ is then destined to live out collectively the
same sequence of images as did Christ. According to Hugo
Rahner, "The earthly fate of the Church as the body of Christ
is modelled on the earthly fate of Christ himself. That is to
say the Church, in the course of her history, moves towards a
death."[4] The death of the Church as a collective carrier of the
process opens up this archetypal cycle to psychological under-

3. Pentecost is considered to be the birthday of the Church.
4. Quoted in Jung, *Mysterium Coniunctionis,* CW 14, par. 28, note 194.

standing and transfers its symbolism to the individual. This is what Jung means by "continuing incarnation."

Insofar as this cycle represents what happens to a man it pictures the process of the ego's coming to consciousness. But, insofar as it represents what happens to God incarnated in man, it pictures the transformation of God.[5] This twofold process has now entered the range of the conscious experience of individuals. Once again the Holy Ghost descends, this time to bring about a "Christification of many."[6] For the individual this means

> not an "imitation of Christ" but its exact opposite: an assimi-
> lation of the Christ-image to his own self. . . . It is no longer
> an effort, an intentional straining after imitation, but rather an
> involuntary experience of the reality represented by the sacred
> legend.[7]

---

5. See Edinger, *The Creation of Consciousness,* pp. 91ff.
6. Jung, "Answer to Job," *Psychology and Religion,* CW 11, par. 758.
7. Jung, *Mysterium Coniunctionis,* CW 14, par. 492.

1

Annunciation

Analysis should release an experience that grips us or falls upon us as from above, an experience that has substance and body such as those things which occurred to the ancients. If I were going to symbolize it I would choose the Annunciation. [1]

---

1. Jung, *Seminar 1925*, p. 111.

1. Annunciation.
(*The Belles Heures of Jean, Duke of Berry*)

AND IN THE SIXTH MONTH[2] THE ANGEL GABRI-
EL WAS SENT FROM GOD UNTO A CITY OF
GALILEE, NAMED NAZARETH. TO A VIRGIN
ESPOUSED TO A MAN WHOSE NAME WAS
JOSEPH, OF THE HOUSE OF DAVID; AND THE
VIRGIN'S NAME WAS MARY. AND THE ANGEL
CAME IN UNTO HER, AND SAID, HAIL, THOU
THAT ART HIGHLY FAVOURED, THE LORD IS
WITH THEE: BLESSED ART THOU AMONG
WOMEN. AND WHEN SHE SAW HIM, SHE WAS
TROUBLED AT HIS SAYING, AND CAST IN HER
MIND WHAT MANNER OF SALUTATION THIS
SHOULD BE. AND THE ANGEL SAID UNTO HER,
FEAR NOT, MARY: FOR THOU HAST FOUND
FAVOUR WITH GOD. AND, BEHOLD, THOU
SHALT CONCEIVE IN THY WOMB, AND BRING
FORTH A SON, AND SHALT CALL HIS NAME
JESUS. HE SHALL BE GREAT, AND SHALL BE
CALLED THE SON OF THE HIGHEST: AND THE
LORD GOD SHALL GIVE UNTO HIM THE THRONE
OF HIS FATHER DAVID; AND HE SHALL REIGN
OVER THE HOUSE OF JACOB FOR EVER; AND OF
HIS KINGDOM THERE SHALL BE NO END. THEN
SAID MARY UNTO THE ANGEL, HOW SHALL
THIS BE, SEEING I KNOW NOT A MAN? AND THE
ANGEL ANSWERED AND SAID UNTO HER, THE
HOLY GHOST SHALL COME UPON THEE, AND
THE POWER OF THE HIGHEST SHALL OVER-
SHADOW THEE; THEREFORE ALSO THAT HOLY
THING WHICH SHALL BE BORN OF THEE SHALL
BE CALLED THE SON OF GOD. AND, BEHOLD,
THY COUSIN ELISABETH, SHE HATH ALSO CON-

2. Of Elisabeth's pregnancy.

CEIVED A SON IN HER OLD AGE: AND THIS IS THE SIXTH MONTH WITH HER, WHO WAS CALLED BARREN. FOR WITH GOD NOTHING SHALL BE IMPOSSIBLE. AND MARY SAID, BEHOLD THE HANDMAID OF THE LORD; BE IT UNTO ME ACCORDING TO THY WORD. AND THE ANGEL DEPARTED FROM HER.   (Luke 1:26-38)[3]

(Frontispiece)

Pictures usually show the Holy Ghost descending as a dove on Mary, indicating that conception occurs simultaneously with the Annunciation. *(Figure 1)* "The Holy Ghost shall come upon thee, and the power of the Highest shall overshadow thee." The word "overshadow" *(episkiazō)* refers to being enveloped in the cloud of the divine presence.[4] The cloud is bright when viewed from the outside but causes darkening when one is enveloped in it *(skia,* shadow, shade). Thus during Christ's transfiguration, "there came a cloud, and overshadowed *[epeskiazen]* them: and they feared as they entered into the cloud."   (Luke 9:34)

Mary's allowing the cloud of Yahweh to rest on her makes her symbolically synonymous with the holy tabernacle in the wilderness or Solomon's temple that houses Yahweh's presence. Gregory Thaumaturgist has God say to the angel of the Annunciation, "Proceed to the sanctuary prepared for me; proceed to the hall of the incarnation; proceed to the pure chamber

3. Unless otherwise indicated, all biblical quotations are from the Authorized (King James) Version.

4. In the Old Testament a cloud is the characteristic manifestation of Yahweh. During the wilderness wandering the Israelites were guided by a pillar of cloud (Exod. 13:21). Yahweh came to Moses on Sinai in a cloud (Exod. 24:15,16). When the tabernacle was set up the cloud covered it (Num. 9:15). When Solomon's temple was completed, "the cloud filled the house of the Lord" (1 Kings 8:10).

of my generation after the flesh. Speak in the ears of my rational [spiritual or symbolic] ark."[5]

The dark aspect of being "overshadowed" by the cloud of Yahweh is not elaborated in canonical material. However Charles Guignebert writes,

> In antiquity, Jews and pagans vied with each other in stories attacking the honor of Mary, who was represented by them as an adulteress, or even a professional prostitute. . . . The Samaritans themselves took part in this offensive chorus. In one of their books . . . [Jesus is described by an expression which] is interpreted by Clermont-Gannean, on the strength of an Arabic translation, as meaning "the son of the courtesan."[6]

Origen speaks of a story reported by Celsus concerning the mother of Jesus which stated that "when she was pregnant she was turned out of doors by the carpenter to whom she had been betrothed, as having been guilty of adultery, and . . . she bore a child to a certain soldier named Panthera."[7]

This legendary material helps to round out the Annunciation considered as a human experience. The dark side of the Annunciation is the fact of an illegitimate pregnancy at a time when adultery might be punished by death. Very few of the innumerable pictures of the Annunciation show the dark aspect of being "overshadowed by the most High."[8] There are some that do so unwittingly by placing the Annunciation side by side with the expulsion of Adam and Eve from the Garden of Eden. These pictures derive from the fact that Mary's obedience to God was often contrasted with Eve's disobedience. In the

5. *The Ante-Nicene Fathers,* vol. 6, p. 66.

6. *Jesus,* pp. 127f.

7. "Origen Against Celsus," 1, 32, *The Ante-Nicene Fathers,* vol. 4, p. 410.

8. An exception is a drawing by Rembrandt *(Figure 2).*

Annunciation by Giovanni di Paolo *(Figure 3)* the dark-winged deity hovers over both the expulsion from the Garden of Eden and the Annunciation.

Paul connects Christ with Adam when he says, "For as in Adam all die, even so in Christ shall all be made alive." (1 Cor. 15:22) Likewise, Mary was connected with Eve by contrast. Justin says,

2. Annunciation. (*Rembrandt drawing*)

3. Annunciation. (*Giovanni di Paolo*)

He (Christ) became man by the Virgin, in order that the dis-obedience which proceeded from the serpent might receive its destruction in the same manner in which it derived its origin. For Eve, who was a virgin and undefiled, having conceived the word of the serpent, brought forth disobedience and death. But the Virgin Mary received faith and joy, when the angel Gabriel announced the good tidings to her that the Spirit of the Lord would come upon her and the power of the Highest would overshadow her.[9]

In the apocryphal *Protevangelium of James,* when Joseph

9. "Dialogue with Trypho," chap. 100, *The Ante-Nicene Fathers,* vol. 1, p. 249.

hears of Mary's pregnancy he exclaims,

> Who has done this evil in my house and defiled her (the virgin)? Has the story (of Adam) been repeated in me? For as Adam was (absent) in the hour of his prayer *and the serpent came and found Eve alone and deceived her* (Gen. 3:1) and defiled her, so also has it happened to me.[10]

Gregory Thaumaturgist says Gabriel is a stand-in for the serpent. "An angel talks with the Virgin in order that the serpent may no more have converse with the woman."[11]

A psychological linkage is established between two images by contrast and opposition as well as by similarity. Eve's obedience to the serpent and Mary's obedience to the angel of the Annunciation are parallel happenings, two symbolic expressions for the same event which are perceived as opposites because they occur at different stages of ego development.

Mary's obedience to the divine call is expressed in her reply, "Behold the handmaid [literally slave-girl] of the Lord; be it unto me according to thy word." Psychologically this signifies the soul's acceptance of its impregnating encounter with the *numinosum*. The consequence of this encounter is the subordination of the ego to the Self, which can feel like slavery.

Hugh of St. Victor interpreted Mary's obedience to God as an expression of love:

> The motive for a conception according to nature is the love of a man for a woman and of a woman for a man. And therefore since a singular love of the Holy Spirit burned in the Virgin's heart, the love of the Holy Spirit wrought great things in her flesh.[12]

Love understood as the urge to individuation constrains both the ego and the Self. Hugh of St. Victor continues:

10. Edgar Hennecke, *New Testament Apocrypha,* vol. 1, p. 381.
11. *The Ante-Nicene Fathers,* vol. 6, p. 65.
12. Jacobus de Voragine, *The Golden Legend,* p. 206.

You have great power, O Love; you alone could draw God
down from heaven to earth. O how strong is your bond with
which even God could be bound. . . . You brought him bound
with your bonds, you brought him wounded with your arrows,
. . . you wounded him who was invulnerable, you bound him
who was invincible, you drew down him who was immovable,
the Eternal you made mortal. . . . O Love, how great is your
victory![13]

The virginity of Mary is an important part of the symbolism.
There seems to be an archetypal connection between virginity
and the ability to handle transpersonal energy (sacred fire). In
ancient Rome the Vestal Virgins were the caretakers of the
sacred flame. Among the Incas of Peru a holy fire was tended
in the temple of the sun by virgins. J.G. Frazer writes,

The Incas of Peru celebrated a festival called Raymi. . . . It
was held in honour of the sun at the solstice in June. For three
days before the festival the people fasted, men did not sleep
with their wives, and no fires were lighted in Cuzco, the
capitol. The sacred new fire was obtained direct from the sun
by concentrating his beams on a highly polished concave plate
and reflecting them on a little cotton wool. . . . Portions of
the new fire were . . . conveyed to the temple of the sun and
to the convent of the sacred virgins, where they were kept
burning all the year and it was an ill omen if the holy flame
went out.[14]

The Apostle Paul says,

There is a difference also between a wife *[gyne]* and a virgin
[parthenos]. The unmarried woman careth for the things of
the Lord, that she may be holy both in body and in spirit; but
she that is married careth for the things of the world, how she
may please her husband.   (1 Cor. 7:34)

13. Quoted in Jung, *Symbols of Transformation*, CW 5, par. 97.
14. "Baldur the Beautiful," *The Golden Bough*, vol. 1, p. 132.

Psychological virginity refers to an attitude which is pure in the sense that it is uncontaminated by personal desirousness. The sacred prostitutes that functioned out of the temples of the Near Eastern love goddess could thus be considered psychological virgins.[15] The virgin ego is one that is sufficiently conscious to relate to transpersonal energies without identifying with them. Philo says, "For the congress of men for the procreation of children makes virgins women. But when God begins to associate with the soul, he brings to pass that she who was formerly woman becomes virgin again."[16] John Donne expresses the paradoxical nature of symbolic chastity. To be virgin means to be God's harlot:

> Batter my heart, three-person'd God . . .
> . . . .
> Take mee to you, imprison mee, for I
> Except you 'enthrall mee, never shall be free,
> Nor ever chast, except you ravish mee.[17]

And according to Angelus Silesius,

> If by God's Holy Ghost thou art beguiled,
> There will be born in thee the Eternal Child.
>
> If it's like Mary, virginal and pure,
> Then God will impregnate your soul for sure.
>
> God make me pregnant, and his Spirit shadow me,
> That God may rise up in my soul and shatter me.
>
> What good does Gabriel's "Ave, Mary" do
> Unless he give me that same greeting too?[18]

15. The meaning of psychological virginity for women is discussed by Esther Harding in *Woman's Mysteries, Ancient and Modern*, pp. 124ff.
16. Quoted in ibid., p. 146.
17. "Holy Sonnets," No. 14.
18. *Cherubinische Wandersmann*, II, 101-104, quoted in Jung, *Mysterium Coniunctionis*, CW 14, par. 444.

2

Nativity

The individual ego is the stable in which the Christ-child is born.[1]

---

1. Remark attributed to Jung.

4. Nativity.
(*The Belles Heures of Jean, Duke of Berry*)

AND IT CAME TO PASS IN THOSE DAYS, THAT
THERE WENT OUT A DECREE FROM CAESAR
AUGUSTUS, THAT ALL THE WORLD SHOULD BE
TAXED. (AND THIS TAXING WAS FIRST MADE
WHEN CYRENIUS WAS GOVERNOR OF SYRIA.)
AND ALL WENT TO BE TAXED, EVERY ONE INTO
HIS OWN CITY. AND JOSEPH ALSO WENT UP
FROM   GALILEE,   OUT   OF   THE   CITY   OF
NAZARETH, INTO JUDAEA, UNTO THE CITY OF
DAVID, WHICH IS CALLED BETHLEHEM; (BE-
CAUSE HE WAS OF THE HOUSE AND LINEAGE
OF DAVID:) TO BE TAXED WITH MARY HIS
ESPOUSED WIFE, BEING GREAT WITH CHILD.
AND SO IT WAS, THAT, WHILE THEY WERE
THERE, THE DAYS WERE ACCOMPLISHED THAT
SHE   SHOULD   BE   DELIVERED.   AND   SHE
BROUGHT FORTH HER FIRSTBORN SON, AND
WRAPPED HIM IN SWADDLING CLOTHES, AND
LAID HIM IN A MANGER; BECAUSE THERE WAS
NO ROOM FOR THEM IN THE INN.   (Luke 2:1-7)

(Figure 4)

The Nativity story begins with the decree that "all the world
should be taxed" (*apographesthai,* registered, enrolled), that
is, a census is taken. An effort to take stock of the totality of
consciousness, the *universus orbis* or circle of the whole
(Vulgate), initiates the birth of the divine child. The earthly
enrollment that precedes the birth of Christ alludes to the "enrollment in heaven" that is a consequence of his coming. As
Christ tells his disciples, "Rejoice not, that the spirits are
subject unto you; but rather rejoice, because your names are
written *[eggegraptai]* in heaven." (Luke 10:20) And in He-
brews the faithful are described as a church of firstborn ones
whose names "are written *[apogegrammenōn]* in heaven."
(12:23)

Although the birth of Christ occurred in Bethlehem, his home town was Nazareth in Galilee. He thus has two cities of origin. This double aspect of his birth leads to the legendary idea that he was twins. Docetism elaborated the notion of a double Jesus—Jesus the human being and Christ the divine spirit that descended on him at baptism, lived through him during his ministry and abandoned him on the cross. The *Pistis Sophia* recounts a story of Jesus' boyhood in which a phantom spirit comes to Mary asking, "Where is Jesus my brother, that I meet with him?" When they were brought together, "he took thee (Jesus) in his arms and kissed thee, and thou also didst kiss him. Ye became one."[2]

According to legend the Messiah will have a double nature:

> The later, mainly Cabalistic tradition speaks of two Messiahs, the Messiah ben Joseph (or ben Ephraim) and the Messiah ben David. They were compared to Moses and Aaron, also to two roes, and this on the authority of the Song of Solomon 4:5: "Thy two breasts are like two young roes that are twins." Messiah ben Joseph is, according to Deuteronomy 32:17, the "firstling of his bullock," and Messiah ben David rides on an ass. Messiah ben Joseph is the first, Messiah ben David the second. Messiah ben Joseph must die in order to "atone with his blood for the children of Yahweh." He will fall in the fight against Gog and Magog, and Armilus will kill him. Armilus is the Anti-Messiah, whom Satan begot on a block of marble. He will be killed by Messiah ben David in his turn. Afterwards, ben David will fetch the new Jerusalem down from heaven and bring ben Joseph back to life. This ben Joseph plays a strange role in later tradition. Tabari, the commentator on the Koran, mentions that the Antichrist will be a king of the Jews, and in Abarbanel's *Mashmi'a Yeshu'ah* the Messiah ben Joseph actually is the Antichrist. So he is not only charac-

---

2. *Pistis Sophia,* ed. and trans. G.R.S. Mead, p. 101.

terized as the suffering Messiah in contrast to the victorious one, but is ultimately thought of as his antagonist.[3]

Messiah ben Joseph corresponds to Jesus born in Nazareth, the personal aspect of the Self. Messiah ben David corresponds to Christ born in Bethlehem, the city of David. He is the son of David the ancestral spirit, the transpersonal aspect of the Self. A parallel image is the Dioscuri Twins, Castor the mortal and Pollux the immortal one.

"And she brought forth her firstborn [*prōtotokos*, first-begotten] son." The "firstborn" have special significance to Yahweh. Unless they are redeemed, bought back, they are to be sacrificed. "Sanctify unto me all the firstborn, whatsoever openeth the womb among the children of Israel, both of man and of beast: it is mine." (Exod. 13:2) It was the firstborn of the Egyptians who were sacrificed to bring about the Exodus. In Psalm 89:27, considered a reference to the Messiah, Yahweh announces, "I will make him my firstborn, higher than the kings of the earth." Paul describes Christ on the one hand as preexistent, "the image of the invisible God, the firstborn of every creature: For by him were all things created" (Col. 1:15,16), and on the other hand as a mortal man who died and yet was resurrected as "the firstborn from the dead." (Col. 1:18) In the latter capacity he is "the firstborn of many brethern" (Rom. 8:29) who will make up a "church of the firstborn . . . [whose names] are written in heaven." (Heb. 12:23)

These references express the paradoxical phenomenology of the Self which is both temporal and eternal, both a sacrificial victim and a ruling king, and which is destined both to die and to be reborn.

The Christ-child was "laid in a manger; because there was

3. Jung, *Aion*, CW 9ii, par. 168.

no room for them in the inn." The term "inn" (*katalyma,* guestchamber) is used on only one other occasion in the New Testament. It appears in the parallel passages of Mark 14:14 and Luke 22:11 in which Christ, in preparation for the Last Supper, sends disciples to inquire, "Where is the guest-chamber *[katalyma],* where I shall eat the passover with my disciples?" The Gnostics used the image of the inn to refer to the "inn of this world." In the Gnostic "Hymn of the Pearl," the incarnating soul similarly descends from heaven to sojourn in "Egypt" and describes itself as "a stranger to my fellow-dwellers in the inn."[4]

There is no room in "this world" for the birth of the Self. It must take place *extra mundum,* since it is an exception, an aberration or even a crime according to the established status quo. If one is not to be a victim of the brute facts of physical existence, he must have a standpoint beyond the "world." "It is possible to have an attitude to the external conditions of life only when there is a point of reference outside them."[5] The birth of the Self brings this point of reference by generating "the incontrovertible experience of an intensely personal, reciprocal relationship between man and an extramundane authority which acts as a counterpoise to the 'world' and its 'reason.'"[6]

Birth among the animals signifies that the coming of the Self is an instinctual process, a part of living nature rooted in the biology of our being. As Jung told a patient, an experience of the transpersonal Self, if it is not to cause inflation, "needs a great humility to counterbalance it. You need to go down to the level of the mice."[7] The junction of the humble and the

4. Hans Jonas, *The Gnostic Religion,* p. 103. See also Edinger, *Ego and Archetype,* pp. 119ff.
5. Jung, "The Undiscovered Self," *Civilization in Transition,* CW 10, par. 506.
6. Ibid., par. 509.
7. *C.G. Jung Speaking,* p. 29.

5. Adoration of the Magi and the Crucifixion. (*Ivory diptych*)

grand is represented by the two sets of visitors who come to worship the Christ-child, the shepherds and the kings or Magi.

According to Matthew 2:1f, "There came wise men from the east to Jerusalem, Saying, Where is he that is born King of the Jews? for we have seen his star in the east and are come to worship him." *(Figure 5)* The number of wise men or Magi is not specified. In early Christian art there may be two or four or occasionally six. In the later Middle Ages the number became fixed at three.[8] In modern dreams the number is more likely to be four.[9] This difference is probably due to the fact that the medieval psyche experienced the sacred images as metaphysical hypostases whereas modern man is now ready to experience them as psychic reality. The "problem of the fourth" always lies between the *idea* of a psychic fact and its experienced reality.

8. James Hall, *Dictionary of Subjects and Symbols in Art*, p. 6.
9. For an example see Edinger, *Ego and Archetype*, p. 126.

The Church Fathers associated the Nativity star with the "star of Jacob" mentioned in Balaam's prophecy: "There shall come a star out of Jacob, and a Sceptre shall rise out of Israel, and shall smite the corners of Moab, and destroy all the children of Sheth." (Num. 24:17) As Jung points out,

> Since olden times, not only among the Jews but all over the Near East, the birth of an outstanding human being has been identified with the rising of a star. . . . Always the hope of a Messiah is connected with the appearance of a star.[10]

Ignatius of Antioch says of the Nativity star,

> A star shone forth in heaven above all that were before it, and its light was inexpressible, while its novelty struck men with astonishment. And all the rest of the stars, with the sun and moon, formed a chorus to this star. It far exceeded them all in brightness.[11]

One star that outshines the others represents "the One Scintilla or monad" among the multiple luminosities of the unconscious and "is to be regarded as a symbol of the self."[12]

The star born in heaven simultaneously with Christ's birth on earth is another example of the double-birth motif. It signifies the transpersonal, cosmic counterpart of Jesus. This theme comes up in modern dreams.[13] The Church established Christmas, the festival of the Nativity, at the winter solstice and thus incorporated the pagan image of the birthday of the new sun, which is symbolically equivalent to the Nativity star.

10. *Aion,* CW 9ii, pars. 179f.
11. "Epistle to the Ephesians," *The Ante-Nicene Fathers,* vol. 1, p. 57.
12. Jung, "On the Nature of the Psyche," *The Structure and Dynamics of the Psyche,* CW 8, par. 388.
13. For examples see Edinger, *Ego and Archetype,* p. 159, and *Anatomy of the Psyche,* pp. 88f.

3

Flight into Egypt

*When a summit of life is reached, when
the bud unfolds and from the lesser the
greater emerges, then, as Nietzsche says,
"One becomes Two," and the greater
figure, which one always was but which
remained invisible, appears to the lesser
personality with the force of a revela-
tion . . . —a moment of deadliest peril!*[1]

1. Jung, "Concerning Rebirth," *The Archetypes and the Collective Unconscious,* CW 9i, par. 217.

6. Flight into Egypt. (*Boucicaut Master*)

BEHOLD, THE ANGEL OF THE LORD APPEARETH
TO JOSEPH IN A DREAM, SAYING, ARISE, AND
TAKE THE YOUNG CHILD AND HIS MOTHER,
AND FLEE INTO EGYPT, AND BE THOU THERE
UNTIL I BRING THEE WORD: FOR HEROD WILL
SEEK THE YOUNG CHILD TO DESTROY HIM.
WHEN HE AROSE, HE TOOK THE YOUNG CHILD
AND HIS MOTHER BY NIGHT, AND DEPARTED
INTO EGYPT. AND WAS THERE UNTIL THE
DEATH OF HEROD: THAT IT MIGHT BE FUL-
FILLED WHICH WAS SPOKEN OF THE LORD BY
THE PROPHET, SAYING, OUT OF EGYPT HAVE I
CALLED MY SON. THEN HEROD, WHEN HE SAW
THAT HE WAS MOCKED OF THE WISE MEN, WAS
EXCEEDING WROTH, AND SENT FORTH, AND
SLEW ALL THE CHILDREN THAT WERE IN
BETHLEHEM, AND IN ALL THE COASTS
THEREOF, FROM TWO YEARS OLD AND UNDER,
ACCORDING TO THE TIME WHICH HE HAD DILI-
GENTLY INQUIRED OF THE WISE MEN. THEN
WAS FULFILLED THAT WHICH WAS SPOKEN BY
JEREMY THE PROPHET, SAYING, IN RAMA WAS
THERE A VOICE HEARD, LAMENTATION, AND
WEEPING, AND GREAT MOURNING, RACHEL
WEEPING FOR HER CHILDREN, AND WOULD
NOT BE COMFORTED, BECAUSE THEY ARE NOT.

(Matt. 2:13-18) *(Figure 6)*

The birth of the hero or divine child is accompanied typically
by threats to its life.[2] The ruling psychic authority (the current
king) is fearful of being superceded by the future king. Thus
the new-born greater authority is always in mortal danger from

2. Cf. the birth of Dionysus, Perseus, Oedipus, Moses, etc.

the ruling dominant of the psyche, just as the latter feels itself in mortal danger from the former.

King Herod is not usually treated sympathetically in artistic representations. An exception is Herod's aria in Berlioz' *L'Enfance du Christ:*

> The dream again! Again the child
> who is to cast me down.
> And not to know what to think
> of this omen which threatens
> my glory and my existence!
> Oh the wretchedness of kings!
> To rule yet not to live,
> to mete out laws to all,
> yet to long to follow
> the goatherd into the heart of the woods!
> Fathomless night
> holding the world
> deep sunk in sleep,
> to my tormented breast
> grant peace for one hour,
> and let thy shadows touch
> my gloom-pressed brow . . .
> Oh the wretchedness of kings, *etc.*
> All effort's useless!
> Sleep shuns me;
> and my vain complaining
> no swifter makes thy course, oh endless night.

Out of this state of mind comes the Massacre of the Innocents. It is in one sense a consequence of Herod's personal fear of being overthrown, but in a deeper sense it is a necessary corollary to the birth of Christ. The birth of the Self is a catastrophic (literally overturning) event, an archetypal dynamism fraught with danger and violence.

Not only must the Holy Family flee to Egypt to avoid Herod's massacre, but also "that it might be fulfilled which was spoken of the Lord by the prophet, saying, Out of Egypt have I called my son." In other words a predetermined (archetypal) pattern is directing the course of events. The reference is to Hosea 11:1: "When Israel was a child, then I loved him, and called my son out of Egypt." This is one of many examples in the New Testament where Christ is made to replace Israel the nation.

In Old Testament usage the nation of Israel is Yahweh's son with whom he deals collectively. The New Testament procedure is to gather up the religious meaning carried collectively by the nation Israel and transfer it to the single figure of Christ, the God-man, who becomes the individual personification of Israel. This is a step toward individual as opposed to collective, group psychology. However the individualizing process remains incomplete since the image of Christ is a unique metaphysical hypostasis. It is now the task of depth psychology to complete the process. The transpersonal meaning carried first collectively by the Jews, then individually by the metaphysical figure of Christ the God-man (still worshiped collectively), is now to be transferred to the psychic experience of individuals.

The Massacre of the Innocents is given an Old Testament precursor in the quotation from Jer. 31:15: "A voice was heard in Ramah, lamentation, and bitter weeping; Rachel weeping for her children refused to be comforted for her children, because they were not." In its original setting this text means that Rachel, their ancestress, weeps for the men of Ephraim, Manasseh and Benjamin massacred or deported by the Assyrians.[3] The passage quoted is immediately followed by a promise of rescue: "Thus saith the Lord; Refrain thy voice from

3. Jerusalem Bible, Matt. 2:17, note g.

weeping, and thine eyes from tears: for thy work shall be rewarded, saith the Lord; and they shall come again from the land of the enemy." (Jer. 31:16)

Christ's flight into and later call out of Egypt is thus foreshadowed not only by Israel's exodus from Egypt but also by her restoration after defeat and captivity as reported by Jeremiah. These foreshadowings illustrate the psychological fact that something new in the psyche can gain admission to consciousness only by following a previously established pattern. Thus it is, for instance, that the new discoveries of depth psychology find entry into the modern mind by the reinterpretation of biblical images.[4]

According to legend, miracles occurred during the journey to Egypt. As the Holy Family passed by, idols toppled from their pedestals *(Figure 7)*, indicating the collapse of false values with the birth of the Self. A wheat field grows miraculously; it is sown in the morning and ready for harvest by afternoon. This story identifies Christ with the vegetation spirit or fertility principle. It also hints at the remarkable phenomenon of temporal aberration that occasionally occurs in the vicinity of the constellated Self. Time and eternity intersect and there may be a brief suspension of the usual categories of consciousness— time, space and causality.

For the Gnostics, Egypt represented "the body," the darkest region of sin and fleshly existence.[5] In the Gnostic "Hymn of the Pearl" the son of the heavenly father descends to Egypt to rescue a pearl from the clutches of a serpent.[6] This is a

---

4. "Any renewal not deeply rooted in the best spiritual tradition is ephemeral; but the dominant that grows from historical roots acts like a living being within the ego-bound man. He does not possess it, it possesses him." (Jung, *Mysterium Coniunctionis,* CW 14, par. 521)
5. Ibid., par. 257.
6. See Edinger, *Ego and Archetype,* pp. 119ff.

7. Flight into Egypt.
(*The Belles Heures of Jean, Duke of Berry*)

coagulatio or incarnation myth,[7] of which the Flight into Egypt is a variation. The fact that the "pearl of great price" is to be found in "Egypt" suggests that the spirit needs a total encounter with matter, that the Self (pearl) requires for realization an Egyptian, earthbound ego.

7. See Edinger, *Anatomy of the Psyche*, pp. 104ff.

4

Baptism

What is it, in the end, that induces a man to go his own way and to rise out of unconscious identity with the mass. . . ? It is what is commonly called vo-cation . . . [which] acts like a law of God from which there is no escape. . . . Anyone with a vocation hears the voice of the inner man: he is called.[1]

1. Jung, "The Development of Personality," *The Development of Person-ality,* CW 17, pars. 299f.

8. Baptism.
(*The Grandes Heures of Jean, Duke of Berry*)

THEN COMETH JESUS FROM GALILEE TO JOR-
DAN UNTO JOHN, TO BE BAPTIZED OF HIM. BUT
JOHN FORBAD HIM, SAYING, I HAVE NEED TO
BE BAPTIZED OF THEE, AND COMEST THOU TO
ME? AND JESUS ANSWERING SAID UNTO HIM,
SUFFER IT TO BE SO NOW: FOR THUS IT
BECOMETH US TO FULFIL ALL RIGHTEOUSNESS.
THEN HE SUFFERED HIM. AND JESUS, WHEN HE
WAS BAPTIZED, WENT UP STRAIGHTWAY OUT
OF THE WATER: AND LO, THE HEAVENS WERE
OPENED UNTO HIM, AND HE SAW THE SPIRIT OF
GOD DESCENDING LIKE A DOVE, AND LIGHTING
UPON HIM: AND LO A VOICE FROM HEAVEN,
SAYING, THIS IS MY BELOVED SON, IN WHOM I
AM WELL PLEASED.   (Matt. 3:13-17) *(Figure 8)*

The baptism of Christ represents an initiation ordeal of sol-
utio,[2] a death and rebirth drama in which the ego encounters
its transpersonal destiny and commits itself to it. For the Church
it is the prototype of the sacrament of baptism which signifies
the death of the old life of the flesh and rebirth into the eternal
life of Christ. As Paul puts it, "We are buried with him by
baptism into death: that like as Christ was raised up from the
dead by the glory of the Father, even so we also should walk
in newness of life." (Rom. 6:4)

His baptism by John indicates that Christ was initially a
follower of John the Baptist. He submitted himself to immer-
sion in the unconscious under the guidance of another. This
was followed by an experience of the autonomous psyche, the
descent of the Holy Spirit. Something similar may happen
when an analysand submits to the transference. What begins
as personal dependence and projection may lead to one's unique

2. See Edinger, *Anatomy of the Psyche,* pp. 47ff.

encounter with the objective psyche. Christ's willingness to submit to baptism by John is explained in the enigmatic phrase, "It becometh us to fulfill all righteousness." I take this to mean that it is just and right initially to submit oneself to the outer authority of another in preparation for the experience of the transpersonal "other" within. One needs a psychological apprenticeship. *(Figure 9)*

According to the Docetist heresy, the divine Christ-nature descended on the man Jesus at his baptism and proceeded to use him as its instrument. Thus, according to Irenaeus, the Gnostics spoke of two baptisms:

> They maintain that those who have attained to perfect knowledge must of necessity be regenerated into that power which is above all. For it is otherwise impossible to find admittance within the Pleroma, since this [regeneration] it is which leads them down into the depths of Bythus. For the baptism instituted by the visible Jesus was for the remission of sins, but the redemption brought in by that Christ who descended upon Him, was for perfection; and they allege that the former is animal, but the latter spiritual. And the baptism of John was proclaimed with a view to repentance, but the redemption by Jesus was brought in for the sake of perfection. And to this He refers when He says, "And I have another baptism to be baptized with, and I hasten eagerly towards it." (Luke 12:30)[3]

The two baptisms correspond psychologically to the baptism of confession (repentance) administered by another, and the baptism of the autonomous psyche in which the individual becomes aware that he must answer to the Self. Thus John the Baptist says, "I indeed baptize you with water unto repentance: but he that cometh after me is mightier than I, whose shoes I am not worthy to bear: he shall baptize you with the Holy Ghost, and with fire." (Matt. 3:11)

3. "Against Heresies," I, XXI, 2, *The Ante-Nicene Fathers,* vol. 1, p. 345.

9. Baptism. (*Rembrandt drawing*)

Several ancient texts mention the presence of fire over the Jordan at the time of Christ's baptism.[4] Justin says, "When Jesus had gone to the river Jordan where John was baptizing, and when He had stepped into the water, a fire was kindled in the Jordan; and when He came out of the water, the Holy Ghost lighted on Him like a dove."[5] The translator says in a note that "the Shechinah probably attended the descent of the Holy Spirit." However, Daniélou puts a different twist on it:

> In this tradition the fire appears to be an allusion to the destructive fire of Judgment, and a number of texts mention it. The following instance occurs in the *Sibylline Oracles:* "After he (the Son of God) has received a second birth according to the

4. See Jean Daniélou, *The Theology of Jewish Christianity,* p. 227.
5. "Dialogue with Trypho," chap. 88, *The Ante-Nicene Fathers,* vol. 1, p. 243.

flesh, being washed in the blue, sluggish stream of Jordan, when he has escaped the fire, he will be the first to see a God coming with good favour by means of the Spirit on the wings of a white dove" (VI, 3-7). The text certainly seems to suggest that Christ was delivered from the fire by baptism, and that it was then that the Spirit descended, a view quite in line with the text of Justin in which the fire appears over the water at the moment when Christ goes down into the Jordan. The idea of Christ's having been delivered at his Baptism from the fire appears elsewhere in the *Oracles,* in a passage which speaks of: "the Father who has spread abroad Thy Baptism in pure water, at which Thou (the Word) didst appear, coming out of the fire" (VII, 83-84).

The same conception occurs in the *Excerpta ex Theodoto.* Clement, giving an account of the teaching of this disciple of Valentinus, writes: "Just as the birth of the Saviour delivered us from the (flux of) becoming and from Fate, so also his Baptism rescued us from the fire and his Passion rescued us from passion" (76,I).[6]

Other texts speak of a "great light."[7]

Understood psychologically, these references indicate that the light and fire of the Shechinah, Yahweh's glory, the fire of the Last Judgment and the dove of the descending Holy Ghost are all aspects of the same phenomenon, namely, the manifestation of the autonomous psyche.[8]

In addition to fire and light, the baptism is accompanied by a voice. The authoritative "voice" appears occasionally in dreams, and calls for the utmost respect.[9] In this case it announces, "This is my beloved Son, in whom I am well pleased." This statement corresponds to a similar one in Isaiah

6. Daniélou, *The Theology of Jewish Christianity,* p. 228.
7. Ibid., p. 230.
8. Fire is associated with calcinatio symbolism. See Edinger, *Anatomy of the Psyche,* pp. 17ff.
9. Jung refers to it in *Psychology and Alchemy,* CW 12, pars. 115 and 294.

42:1 which proclaims the "Servant of Yahweh": "Behold my servant, whom I uphold; mine elect, in whom my soul delighteth; I have put my spirit upon him." It conveys the message that the ego, as it accepts its vocation and destiny, has the love and support of the Self.

In Psalm 74:13 we read, "Thou didst divide the sea by thy strength: thou brakest the heads of the dragons in the waters." Cyril of Jerusalem applied this text to Christ's baptism: "Since, therefore, it was necessary to break the heads of the dragon in pieces, He went down and bound the strong ones in the waters."[10] Daniélou notes that "the theme of the dragon hidden in the waters of death, and of Christ's baptism as a descent into the dragon's domain was to endure in tradition."[11] From this follows the remarkable idea that Christ's baptism brought about a cleansing of water by destroying "the demonic forces that dwelt in it."[12] Ignatius writes, "He was born and baptized, that by His passion He might purify the water,"[13] and Clement of Alexandria says,

> The Lord had himself baptised, not that he had need of it for himself, but so that he might sanctify all water for those that are regenerated in it. In this way not only are our bodies cleansed but our souls also, and the sanctification of the invisible parts of our being is signified by the fact that even the impure spirits which cleave to our soul, are rooted out from the time of the new spiritual birth.[14]

The idea of the cleansing and sanctification of water suggests

10. "Cathechetical Lectures," III, II, quoted in Daniélou, *The Theology of Jewish Christianity,* p. 225.

11. Ibid.

12. Ibid., p. 226.

13. "Epistle to the Ephesians," chap. 18, *The Ante-Nicene Fathers,* vol. 1, p. 57.

14. "Eclogae Propheticae," 7, quoted in Daniélou, *The Theology of Jewish Christianity,* p. 227.

the transformation of the unconscious itself. What had once been the abode of demons (autonomous complexes that threaten to possess the ego) may, through increasing consciousness, be experienced as the sacred, transpersonal ground of being.

Christ's Baptism signifies his encounter with destiny. It is simultaneously an active commitment and a passive anointing by John and by the Holy Spirit. In the psychology of individuation destiny and identity are the same, expressed by the twin questions, "What am I?" and "Who am I?"[15] John the Baptist as the forerunner who "prepares a way for the Lord" (Matt. 3:3) is the bringer of this question. While imprisoned by Herod he sent to Christ this question: "Art thou he that should come, or do we look for another?" (Matt. 11:3) Christ's answer is a model of canniness:

> Go and shew John again those things which ye do hear and see: The blind receive their sight, and the lame walk, the lepers are cleansed, and the deaf hear, the dead are raised up, and the poor have the gospel preached to them. (Matt. 11:4,5)

This answer avoids explicit identification with the Self while acknowledging its presence by reference to its effects, namely, insight, perception, healing and renewed vitality.

"Are you the one?" is the crucial question of individuation. Once it is asked[16] the die is cast and the process must live itself out for good or ill. The Gnostics attempted to engage this question and answered it in their famous formula, "What

---

15. *Quis* (who) or *quid* (what) distinguishes the personal from the impersonal and objective. "Quis refers to the ego, quid to the self." (Jung, *Mysterium Coniunctionis,* CW 14, par. 362, note 51)

16. "Fortunately, in her kindness and patience, Nature never puts the fatal question as to the meaning of their lives into the mouths of most people. And where no one asks, no one need answer." (Jung, "The Development of the Personality," *The Development of the Personality,* CW 17, par. 314)

liberates is the knowledge of who we were, what we became; where we were, where into we have been thrown; whereto we speed, wherefrom we are redeemed; what birth is, and what rebirth."[17]

Immediately following the Baptism we read, "Then was Jesus led up of the Spirit into the wilderness to be tempted of the devil." (Matt. 4:1) This sequence refers to the danger of inflation that accompanies an encounter with the Self. The Holy Spirit that blessed Christ turns diabolical and becomes the tempter. This image expresses the ego's temptation to identify with the transpersonal energy and use it for the purposes of personal power.

> The story of the Temptation clearly reveals the nature of the psychic power with which Jesus came into collision: it was the power-intoxicated devil of the prevailing Caesarean psychology that led him into dire temptation in the wilderness. This devil was the objective psyche that held all the peoples of the Roman Empire under its sway, and that is why it promised Jesus all the kingdoms of the earth, as if it were trying to make a Caesar of him. Obeying the inner call of his vocation, Jesus voluntarily exposed himself to the assaults of the imperialistic madness that filled everyone, conqueror and conquered alike. In this way he recognized the nature of the objective psyche which had plunged the whole world into misery and had begotten a yearning for salvation that found expression even in the pagan poets. Far from suppressing or allowing himself to be suppressed by this psychic onslaught, he let it act on him consciously, and assimilated it. Thus was world-conquering Caesarism transformed into spiritual kingship, and the Roman Empire into the universal kingdom of God that was not of this world.[18]

17. Hans Jonas, *The Gnostic Religion,* p. 45.
18. Jung, "The Development of the Personality," *The Development of the Personality,* CW 17, par. 309.

5

Triumphal Entry into Jerusalem

We all must do just what Christ did. We must make our experiment. We must make mistakes. We must live out our own vision of life. And there will be error. If you avoid error you do not live.[1]

---

1. Jung, *C.G. Jung Speaking*, p. 98.

10. Triumphal Entry.
(*The Grandes Heures of Jean, Duke of Berry*)

AND WHEN THEY DREW NIGH UNTO JERUSALEM, AND WERE COME TO BETHPHAGE, UNTO THE MOUNT OF OLIVES, THEN SENT JESUS TWO DISCIPLES, SAYING UNTO THEM, GO INTO THE VILLAGE OVER AGAINST YOU, AND STRAIGHTWAY YE SHALL FIND AN ASS TIED, AND A COLT WITH HER: LOOSE THEM, AND BRING THEM UNTO ME. AND IF ANY MAN SAY OUGHT UNTO YOU, YE SHALL SAY, THE LORD HATH NEED OF THEM; AND STRAIGHTWAY HE WILL SEND THEM. ALL THIS WAS DONE, THAT IT MIGHT BE FULFILLED WHICH WAS SPOKEN BY THE PROPHET, SAYING, TELL YE THE DAUGHTER OF SION, BEHOLD, THY KING COM-ETH UNTO THEE, MEEK, AND SITTING UPON AN ASS, AND A COLT THE FOAL OF AN ASS. AND THE DISCIPLES WENT, AND DID AS JESUS COM-MANDED THEM, AND BROUGHT THE ASS, AND THE COLT, AND PUT ON THEM THEIR CLOTHES, AND THEY SET HIM THEREON. AND A VERY GREAT MULTITUDE SPREAD THEIR GARMENTS IN THE WAY; OTHERS CUT DOWN BRANCHES FROM THE TREES, AND STRAWED THEM IN THE WAY. AND THE MULTITUDES THAT WENT BEFORE, AND THAT FOLLOWED, CRIED, SAY-ING, HOSANNA TO THE SON OF DAVID: BLESSED IS HE THAT COMETH IN THE NAME OF THE LORD; HOSANNA IN THE HIGHEST. (Matt. 21:1-9)

(Figure 10)

The culminating drama of Christ's life begins with "that strange incident, the triumphal entry into Jerusalem."[2] At this

2. Ibid., p. 97.

moment he succumbs to the power temptation and allows himself to be hailed as a king. And no sooner does he enter Jerusalem than he falls into a rage.

> AND JESUS WENT INTO THE TEMPLE OF GOD, AND CAST OUT ALL THEM THAT SOLD AND BOUGHT IN THE TEMPLE, AND OVERTHREW THE TABLES OF THE MONEYCHANGERS, AND THE SEATS OF THEM THAT SOLD DOVES, AND SAID UNTO THEM, IT IS WRITTEN, MY HOUSE SHALL BE CALLED THE HOUSE OF PRAYER; BUT YE HAVE MADE IT A DEN OF THIEVES.
>
> (Matt. 21:12,13) *(Figure 11)*

The bad mood continues on the following day when he curses a fig tree because it had no fruit to offer him. (Matt. 21:19)

His manner of entry into Jerusalem indicates that Christ explicitly identifies himself with the Messianic king foretold in Zechariah 9:9.

> Rejoice greatly, O daughter of Zion; shout, O daughter of Jerusalem: behold, thy King cometh unto thee: he is just, and having salvation; lowly, and riding upon an ass, and upon a colt the foal of an ass.

Overt identification with an archetypal image is exceedingly dangerous and yet Christ's destiny seems to require it as the dark aspect of the incarnation process. His anger against the moneychangers violates his own injunction against anger (Matt. 5:22) and indicates that "money" was an aspect of his shadow. However this onesidedness was necessary as part of his destined task to set up a spiritual "kingdom" over and against the crude materialism of the time. As Jung says, in the Temptation, "Jesus voluntarily exposed himself to the

11. Christ Driving the Moneychangers from the Temple.
(Rembrandt etching)

assaults [from within] of the imperialistic madness that filled
everyone, conqueror and conquered alike."[3]

Exposure of the ego to such unconscious forces always gen-
erates some degree of possession or identification, even if only
partial and temporary. Also the transformation drama cannot
unfold without the ego's succumbing to "necessary error" *(felix
culpa)*.[4]

3. "The Development of the Personality," *The Development of the Personality,* CW 17, par. 309.
4. "Egocentricity is a necessary attribute of consciousness and is also its
   specific sin." (Jung, *Mysterium Coniunctionis,* CW 14, par. 364)

6

Last Supper

If the projected conflict is to be healed, it must return into the psyche of the individual, where it had its unconscious beginnings. He must celebrate a Last Supper with himself, and eat his own flesh and drink his own blood; which means that he must recognize and accept the other in himself. . . . Is this perhaps the meaning of Christ's teaching, that each must bear his own cross? For if you have to endure yourself, how will you be able to rend others also?[1]

---

1. Jung, *Mysterium Coniunctionis*, CW 14, par. 512.

12. Last Supper.
(*The Hours of Catherine of Cleves*)

AND AS THEY WERE EATING, JESUS TOOK
BREAD, AND BLESSED IT, AND BRAKE IT, AND
GAVE IT TO THE DISCIPLES, AND SAID, TAKE,
EAT; THIS IS MY BODY. AND HE TOOK THE CUP,
AND GAVE THANKS, AND GAVE IT TO THEM,
SAYING, DRINK YE ALL OF IT; FOR THIS IS MY
BLOOD OF THE NEW TESTAMENT, WHICH IS
SHED FOR MANY FOR THE REMISSION OF SINS.

(Matt. 26:26,27)

WHOSO EATETH MY FLESH, AND DRINKETH MY
BLOOD, HATH ETERNAL LIFE.   (John 6:54)

(Figure 12)

The image of the Last Supper has undergone enormous
symbolic development because its reenactment became the
central rite of the Christian Church. Jung has written a major
essay on this subject.[2] He observes,

> Although the Mass itself is a unique phenomenon in the history
> of comparative religion, its symbolic content would be pro-
> foundly alien to man were it not rooted in the human psyche.
> But if it is so rooted, then we may expect to find similar
> patterns of symbolism both in the earlier history of mankind
> and in the world of pagan thought contemporary with it. . . .
> The liturgy of the Mass contains allusions to the "prefigura-
> tions" in the Old Testament, and thus indirectly to ancient
> sacrificial symbolism in general. It is clear, then, that in Christ's
> sacrifice and the Communion one of the deepest chords in the
> human psyche is struck: human sacrifice and ritual
> anthropophagy. . . . I must content myself with mentioning
> the ritual slaying of the king to promote the fertility of the
> land and the prosperity of his people, the renewal and revivifi-

2. "Transformation Symbolism in the Mass," *Psychology and Religion,*
   CW 11.

cation of the gods through human sacrifice, and the totem meal, the purpose of which was to reunite the participants with the life of their ancestors. These hints will suffice to show how the symbols of the Mass penetrate into the deepest layers of the psyche and its history.[3]

The Last Supper is a particular example of the "banquet" archetype or sacred meal and thus belongs to the larger category of coagulatio symbolism.[4] The first Last Supper was a Passover meal and thus assimilates Passover symbolism to itself. Christ replaces the Paschal lamb as the redeeming sacrifical victim. (Exod. 12:3ff) The "totem meal" aspect of the Last Supper is illustrated by its parallel to the Dionysian rite of *Omophagia*, "the feast of raw flesh." Clement of Alexandria says, "The Bacchoi hold orgies in honor of a mad Dionysus, they celebrate a divine madness by the Eating of Raw Flesh, the final accomplishment of their rite is the distribution of the flesh of butchered victims."[5] Jane Harrison tells us, "An integral part of this terrible ritual was the tearing asunder of the slain beast [bull or goat] in order, no doubt, to get the flesh as raw as might be, for the blood is the life."[6] This ritual reenacted the dismemberment and eating of the infant Dionysus by the Titans.

There are striking parallels between the myths of Christ and Dionysus. Dionysus was the only god in the Greek pantheon to be born of a mortal woman, Semele. He rescued his mother from Hades and had her installed in heaven. In his first life he was dismembered as an infant by the Titans and thus experi-

---

3. Ibid., par. 339.
4. See Edinger, *Anatomy of the Psyche,* pp. 111ff.
5. "Exhortation to the Greeks," II, 12, quoted in Jane Harrison, *Prolegomena to the Study of Greek Religion,* p. 483.
6. Ibid., pp. 482f.

enced a "passion." In the *Omophagia* Dionysus offers his worshipers his own flesh to eat as warrant of their immortality. The tragic drama is an outgrowth of the Dionysian mysteries and parallels the tragic view of life in "this world" as developed by Christianity.[7]

In the *Omophagia* the sacrificed bull or goat represents Dionysus himself who offers his devotees his own flesh to eat. Similarly, at the Last Supper and in the ritual of the Mass, Christ offers his body and blood for the spiritual nourishment of believers. In this context Christ represents the Anthropos, the original whole man. To partake of his flesh means to partake of the eternal and transpersonal. As Jung says,

> The mystery of the Eucharist transforms the soul of the empirical man, who is only a part of himself, into his totality, symbolically expressed by Christ. In this sense, therefore, we can speak of the Mass as the *rite of the individuation process.*[8]

Just as Christ tells his disciples, "Whoso eateth my flesh and drinketh my blood hath eternal life,"[9] so participation in the *Omophagia* renders the worshiper a *Bacchos,* that is, invests him with the divine nature of Dionysus.[10] The flesh of Christ or Dionysus is thus a *cibus immortalis* (food of immortality) which is also a synonym for the Philosophers' Stone.[11] Psychologically this means consciousness of the Self which allows one to see things "under the aspect of eternity."

7. Christ and Dionysus also share wine and grape symbolism. See Edinger, *Ego and Archetype,* pp. 235ff.
8. "Transformation Symbolism in the Mass," *Psychology and Religion,* CW 11, par. 414.
9. John 6:56 adds, "He that eateth my flesh, and drinketh my blood, dwelleth in me, and I in him."
10. See Harrison, *Prolegomena to the Study of Greek Religion,* pp. 478ff.
11. Jung, *Mysterium Coniunctionis,* CW 14, par. 525.

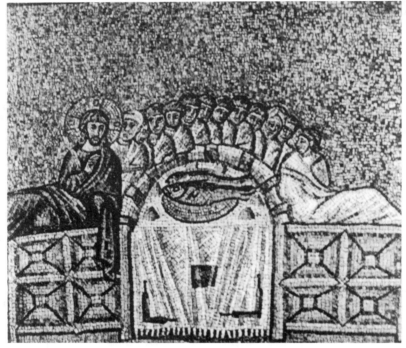

13. Early Christian Last Supper. (*Mosaic*)

In early iconography the Last Supper was pictured as a fish meal. *(Figure 13)* Christ himself was equated with a fish *(ichthys)*.[12] This symbolism connects the Last Supper with the Messianic Banquet of Jewish legend which is also a fish meal, one in which the flesh of Leviathan, the sea monster, will be served to the pious.[13] Eating Leviathan is a clear reference to conscious *assimilation* of the primordial psyche. The same

12. Christ as fish is discussed at length by Jung in "The Sign of the Fishes," *Aion*, CW 9ii, pars. 127ff.
13. Raphael Patai, *The Messiah Texts,* pp. 236f.

implication applies to the Last Supper as a fish meal. Fish represent unconscious contents of a cold-blooded, concupiscent nature. Like Leviathan, the great fish, they are smaller versions of the primordial psyche which requires transformation by conscious realization.[14]

These considerations reveal the paradoxical nature of Eucharistic symbolism. On the one hand the "food" provides a redeeming connection with the transpersonal Self. On the other hand it is the *prima materia* which must be transformed and humanized by the efforts of the ego. Paul was aware of the dual nature of the Eucharist when he wrote, "Let a man examine himself, and so let him eat of that bread, and drink of that cup. For he that eateth and drinketh unworthily, eateth and drinketh damnation to himself, not discerning the Lord's body." (1 Cor. 11:28,29)

14. Cf. the apocryphal Book of Tobit.

7

Gethsemane

The problem of crucifixion is the beginning of individuation; there is the secret meaning of the Christian symbolism, a path of blood and suffering.[1]

---

1. Jung, unpublished letter, quoted in Gerhard Adler, "Aspects of Jung's Personality and Work," p. 12. Cf. Nikos Kazantzakis, *The Saviors of God,* p. 93: "We discern a crimson line on this earth, a red, blood-spattered line which ascends, struggling, from matter to plants, from plants to animals, from animals to man."

14. Agony in the Garden.
(*The Hours of Catherine of Cleves*)

THEN COMETH JESUS WITH THEM UNTO A
PLACE CALLED GETHSEMANE, AND SAITH
UNTO THE DISCIPLES, SIT YE HERE, WHILE I GO
AND PRAY YONDER. AND HE TOOK WITH HIM
PETER AND THE TWO SONS OF ZEBEDEE, AND
BEGAN TO BE SORROWFUL AND VERY HEAVY.
THEN SAITH HE UNTO THEM, MY SOUL IS
EXCEEDING SORROWFUL, EVEN UNTO DEATH:
TARRY YE HERE, AND WATCH WITH ME. AND
HE WENT A LITTLE FURTHER, AND FELL ON HIS
FACE, AND PRAYED, SAYING, O MY FATHER, IF
IT BE POSSIBLE, LET THIS CUP PASS FROM ME:
NEVERTHELESS NOT AS I WILL, BUT AS THOU
WILT. AND HE COMETH UNTO THE DISCIPLES,
AND FINDETH THEM ASLEEP, AND SAITH UNTO
PETER, WHAT, COULD YE NOT WATCH WITH ME
ONE HOUR? WATCH AND PRAY, THAT YE ENTER
NOT INTO TEMPTATION: THE SPIRIT INDEED IS
WILLING, BUT THE FLESH IS WEAK. HE WENT
AWAY AGAIN THE SECOND TIME, AND PRAYED,
SAYING, O MY FATHER, IF THIS CUP MAY NOT
PASS AWAY FROM ME, EXCEPT I DRINK IT, THY
WILL BE DONE. AND HE CAME AND FOUND
THEM ASLEEP AGAIN: FOR THEIR EYES WERE
HEAVY. AND HE LEFT THEM, AND WENT AWAY
AGAIN, AND PRAYED THE THIRD TIME, SAYING
THE SAME WORDS.   (Matt. 26:36-44)

AND THERE APPEARED AN ANGEL UNTO HIM
FROM HEAVEN, STRENGTHENING HIM. AND
BEING IN AN AGONY HE PRAYED MORE EAR-
NESTLY: AND HIS SWEAT WAS AS IT WERE
GREAT DROPS OF BLOOD FALLING DOWN TO
THE GROUND.   (Luke 22:43,44) *(Figure 14)*

In Gethsemane Christ faces fully the terrible realization that he is destined to be crucified. This destiny is symbolized by the image of the "cup" *(potērion)*. In the Old Testament this term has two chief usages: the cup of divination from which one draws lots to determine one's destined portion, and the cup of Yahweh's wrath. The Psalmist exclaims, "The Lord is the portion of mine inheritance and of my cup: thou maintainest my lot." (Ps. 16:5) Isaiah announces, "Awake, awake, stand up, O Jerusalem, which hast drunk at the hand of the Lord the cup of his fury; thou hast drunken the dregs of the cup of trembling, and wrung them out." (Isa. 51:17)[2] It is Christ's destined task to drink to the dregs the cup of Yahweh's wrath. And terrible wrath it is that requires for its satisfaction the torture and death of his own son. Psychologically this means that it is the ego's task in individuation to assimilate the affects of the primordial psyche.

In medieval pictures (e.g., *Figure 14*) Christ is often represented as accepting a communion cup and wafer from the hand of God, that is, he is eating and drinking his own flesh and blood. Gethsemane thus completes the symbolism of the Last Supper.[3] This process corresponds to the ancient image of the uroboros, the snake that devours its own tail:

> In the age-old image of the uroboros lies the thought of devouring oneself and turning oneself into a circulatory process. . . . The uroboros is a dramatic symbol for the integration and assimilation of the opposite, i.e., of the shadow. This "feed-back" process is at the same time a symbol of immortal-

---

2. See also Ps. 75:8; Jer. 13:13, 25:15-18, 48:26, 49:12, 51:7; Lam. 4:21; Ezek. 23:32-34; Hab. 2:15-16; Zech. 12:2.

3. Chrysostom said that "Christ was the first to eat his own flesh and drink his own blood (at the institution of the Last Supper)." (Jung, *Mysterium Coniunctionis,* CW 14, par. 423)

ity. . . . He symbolizes the One, who proceeds from the clash of opposites.[4]

Christ's willingness to drink the cup of Yahweh's wrath has the effect of "digesting" Yahweh's evil, thereby transforming him into a loving God. Anyone who assimilates a bit of the collective or archetypal shadow is contributing to the transformation of God.[5] Erich Neumann puts it this way:

> To the extent that he does live in reality the whole range of his particular life, the individual is . . . an alchemical retort, in which the elements present in the collective are melted down and refashioned to form a new synthesis, which is then offered to the collective. But the predigestion of evil which he carried out as part of the process of assimilating his shadow makes him, at the same time, an agent for the immunization of the collective. An individual's shadow is invariably bound up with the collective shadow of his group, and as he digests his own evil, a fragment of the collective evil is invariably co-digested at the same time.[6]

The Gethsemane experience is plagued by sleepiness. Three of the four figures sleep through the whole event although Christ pleads with them to stay awake and watch (*grēgoreō,* be alert and vigilant). The same term is used by the apocalyptic Christ in Rev. 16:15: "Behold, I come as a thief. Blessed is he that watcheth *[ho grēgorōn].*" The emphasis on wakefulness indicates that the issue at stake is consciousness. Christ is going through an *agonia* which is not just an agony but also an *agone,* a contest or conflict between flesh and spirit.

The message seems to be that to survive the conflict between

4. Ibid., par. 513.
5. See Edinger, *The Creation of Consciousness,* pp. 91ff.
6. *Depth Psychology and a New Ethic,* p. 130.

the opposites one must either sleep or pray. As a psychological procedure prayer corresponds to active imagination, whereby one seeks to bring into visibility the psychic image or fantasy that lies behind the conflict of affects.[7] The emerging image often has a redeeming or transforming effect which reconciles the conflicting opposites.

The source of inner strength constellated by prayer or active imagination is personified in Luke by the ministering angel. *(Figure 15)* This state of affairs is described in the lines of Hölderlin:

> Where danger is,
> Grows also the rescuing power.[8]

Or, as Jung puts it,

> The highest and most decisive experience of all . . . is to be alone with . . . [one's] own self, or whatever else one chooses to call the objectivity of the psyche. The patient must be alone if he is to find out what it is that supports him when he can no longer support himself. Only this experience can give him an indestructible foundation.[9]

Concerning the conflict between flesh and spirit which occurs at Gethsemane, Origen makes an interesting observation:

> Of the passages in the gospels which concern the soul of the Saviour, it is noticeable that some refer to it under the name

---

7. See Jung, *Memories, Dreams, Reflections,* p. 177: "To the extent that I managed to translate the emotions into images—that is to say, to find the images which were concealed in the emotions—I was inwardly calmed and reassured. Had I left those images hidden in the emotions, I might have been torn to pieces by them. . . . As a result of my experiment I learned how helpful it can be, from the therapeutic point of view, to find the particular images which lie behind emotions."

8. *Wo aber Gefahr ist, / Wächst das Rettende auch.* ("Patmos")

9. *Psychology and Alchemy,* CW 12, par. 32.

15. Christ Consoled by an Angel.
(*Rembrandt etching*)

of soul and others under the name of spirit. When scripture wishes to indicate any suffering or trouble that affected him, it does so under the name soul, as when it says: "Now is my soul troubled," and "My soul is sorrowful even unto death," and "No one taketh my soul from me, but I lay it down of myself." On the other hand he commends "into his Father's hands" not his soul but his spirit; and when he says the "flesh is weak" he does not say the "soul" is "willing" but the "spirit"; from which it appears as if the soul were a kind of medium between the weak flesh and the willing spirit.[10]

In the suffering of Gethsemane the conflict between body and spirit is reconciled in the psyche, the medium that unites them.[11] This is an extraction procedure,[12] its product the bloody sweat, corresponding to the *aqua permanens* of the alchemists. A text by the alchemist Gerhard Dorn illustrates the parallel:

[The philosophers] called their stone animate because, at the final operations, by virtue of the power of this most noble fiery mystery, a dark red liquid, like blood, sweats out drop by drop from their material and their vessel. And for this reason they have prophesied that in the last days a most pure [or genuine] man, through whom the world will be freed, will come to earth and will sweat bloody drops of a rosy or red hue, whereby the world will be redeemed from its Fall. In like manner, too, the blood of their stone will free the leprous metals and also men from their diseases. . . . and that is the reason why the stone is called animate. For in the blood of this stone is hidden its soul. . . . For a like reason they have called it their microcosm, because it contains the similitude of all things of this world,

10. *Origen on First Principles,* pp. 127f.
11. "Every psychic advance of man arises from the suffering of the soul." (Jung, "Psychotherapists or the Clergy," *Psychology and Religion,* CW 11, par. 497)
12. "Gethsemane" means "oil press," a place for the extraction of olive oil.

and therefore again they say that it is animate, as Plato calls the macrocosm animate.[13]

Jung gives the following commentary to Dorn's text:

Since the stone represents the *homo totus,* it is only logical for Dorn to speak of the "putissimus homo" [most true man] when discussing the arcane substance and its bloody sweat, for this is what it is all about. *He* is the arcanum, and the stone and its parallel or prefiguration is Christ in the garden of Gethsemane. This "most pure" or "most true" man must be no other than what he is, just as "argentum putum" is unalloyed silver; he must be entirely man, a man who knows and possesses everything human and is not adulterated by any influence or admixture from without. This man will appear on earth only "in the last days." He cannot be Christ, for Christ by his blood has already redeemed the world from the consequences of the Fall. . . . On no account is it a question here of a future Christ and *salvator microcosmi,* but rather of the alchemical *servator cosmi* (preserver of the cosmos), representing the still unconscious idea of the whole and complete man, who shall bring about what the sacrificial death of Christ has obviously left unfinished, namely the deliverance of the world from evil. Like Christ he will sweat a redeeming blood, but . . . it is "rose-colored"; not natural or ordinary blood, but symbolic blood, a psychic substance, the manifestation of a certain kind of Eros which unifies the individual as well as the multitude in the sign of the rose and makes them whole.[14]

13. Quoted in Jung, "The Philosophical Tree," *Alchemical Studies,* CW 13, par. 381.
14. Ibid., par. 390.

8

Arrest and Trial

*He said "My kingdom is not of this
world." But "kingdom" it was, all the
same.*[1]

1. *C.G. Jung Speaking*, p. 97.

16. Taking of Christ.
(*The Hours of Catherine of Cleves*)

ARREST

BEHOLD, THE HOUR IS AT HAND, AND THE SON OF MAN IS BETRAYED INTO THE HANDS OF SIN-NERS. RISE, LET US BE GOING: BEHOLD, HE IS AT HAND THAT DOTH BETRAY ME. AND WHILE HE YET SPAKE, LO, JUDAS, ONE OF THE TWELVE, CAME, AND WITH HIM A GREAT MUL-TITUDE WITH SWORDS AND STAVES, FROM THE CHIEF PRIESTS AND ELDERS OF THE PEOPLE. NOW HE THAT BETRAYED HIM GAVE THEM A SIGN, SAYING, WHOMSOEVER I SHALL KISS, THAT SAME IS HE: HOLD HIM FAST. AND FORTH-WITH HE CAME TO JESUS, AND SAID, HAIL, MAS-TER; AND KISSED HIM. AND JESUS SAID UNTO HIM, FRIEND, WHEREFORE ART THOU COME? THEN CAME THEY, AND LAID HANDS ON JESUS, AND TOOK HIM.   (Matt. 26:45-50) *(Figure 16)*

The tragic drama now hastens to its end with Christ's encounter with the hostile "multitude." This term (*ochlos,* crowd, mob) refers to "an unorganized multitude, in contrast to *demos,* the people as a body politic."[2] The corresponding verb, *ochleō,* means "to disturb by a mob or tumult . . . to be troublesome."[3] It refers to collective man or "mass man," who is boisterous, demanding and inclined to riot.

Crowds have been mentioned earlier in the Gospel account, for example Matthew 4:25: "And there followed him great crowds of people *[ochloi].*" Again at the Triumphal Entry into Jerusalem, "and a very great multitude *[ochlos]* spread their

2. W.E. Vine, *An Expository Dictionary of New Testament Words,* vol. 3, p. 91.
3. Liddel and Scott, *Greek-English Lexicon,* p. 509.

garments in the way. . . . And the multitudes *[ochloi]* that went before, and that followed, cried, saying, Hosanna to the Son of David." (Matt. 21:8,9) We cannot avoid the impression that with the Triumphal Entry Christ "played to the crowd" in the sense that he accepted its collective projection of the "Son of David," an explicit reference to the Messiah.

All collectivities are unconscious psychic organisms of great power and danger. They embody archetypal energies without the mediation of a conscious ego and hence are notoriously fickle. "The bigger the crowd the more negligible the individual becomes,"[4] but "the carrier of . . . consciousness is the individual."[5] Jung adds, "Did Christ, perchance, call his disciples to him at a mass meeting? Did the feeding of the five thousand bring him any followers who did not afterwards cry with the rest 'Crucify him!' . . . ?"[6] And, we might add, was not the "crowd" that hailed him "Son of David" the same one that afterwards cried "Crucify him!" when it learned that his kingdom was "not of this world?"

With the arrest of Christ not only does the fickle crowd betray him, which is to be expected, but also one of his disciples. Betrayal is a theme of individuation because it pertains to the phenomenology of the opposites. It is another word for enantiodromia.[7] In a situation of conflict between opposing values an individual reverses allegiance and opens the gates to the enemy. The traitor has always been despised by both

4. Jung, "The Undiscovered Self," *Civilization in Transition,* CW 10, par. 503.
5. Ibid., par. 528.
6. Ibid., par. 536.
7. "Enantiodromia means a 'running counter to.' In the philosophy of Heraclitus it is used to designate the play of opposites in the course of events—the view that everything that exists turns into its opposite." (Jung, "Definitions," *Psychological Types,* CW 6, par. 708)

sides because he violates a "sacred" value of collective psychology, namely, fidelity to identity with the group.

Loyalty and betrayal are a pair of opposites. Loyalty to the future may require betrayal of the past or vice versa. In a sense, Christ betrayed his collective Jewish heritage. He was a heretic and therefore was punished as a traitor. This corresponds to the psychological fact that at a certain stage of development the individual may be obliged to betray collective loyalties to achieve individuation. Later, the fruits of that "crime" may become a contribution to the collective.

According to John 13:26f Judas is given his terrible fate at the Last Supper. After Christ announces that one of his disciples will betray him, he is asked who it will be. He replies, "He it is, to whom I shall give a sop, when I have dipped it. And when he had dipped the sop, he gave it to Judas Iscariot, the son of Simon. And after the sop Satan entered into him."

Certain medieval pictures show Satan as a tiny demon entering the mouth of Judas as Christ gives him a morsel. *(Figure 12)* It is as though Christ fed Judas his assigned destiny at that moment and Judas dutifully carried it out. This may explain why the betrayal is accomplished with a "kiss" and why Christ calls Judas "friend" as he receives the kiss. It is an act of love to lead a person to his proper destiny. It was Christ's destiny to be crucified. Therefore he calls Judas "friend" and reacts angrily when Peter suggests he could avoid that fate:

> Jesus began to make it clear to his disciples that he was destined to go to Jerusalem and suffer grievously at the hands of the elders and chief priests and scribes, to be put to death and to be raised up on the third day. Then, taking him aside, Peter started to remonstrate with him. "Heaven preserve you, Lord;" he said. "This must not happen to you." But he turned and said to Peter, "Get behind me, Satan! You are an obstacle in my path, because the way you think is not God's way but man's." (Matt. 16:21-23, Jerusalem Bible)

TRIAL BEFORE CAIAPHAS

AND THEY THAT HAD LAID HOLD ON JESUS LED
HIM AWAY TO CAIAPHAS THE HIGH PRIEST,
WHERE THE SCRIBES AND THE ELDERS WERE
ASSEMBLED. . . . NOW THE CHIEF PRIESTS,
AND ELDERS, AND ALL THE COUNCIL, SOUGHT
FALSE WITNESS AGAINST JESUS, TO PUT HIM
TO DEATH; BUT FOUND NONE: YEA, THOUGH
MANY FALSE WITNESSES CAME, YET FOUND
THEY NONE. AT THE LAST CAME TWO FALSE
WITNESSES, AND SAID, THIS FELLOW SAID, I
AM ABLE TO DESTROY THE TEMPLE OF GOD,
AND TO BUILD IT IN THREE DAYS. AND THE
HIGH PRIEST AROSE, AND SAID UNTO HIM,
ANSWEREST THOU NOTHING? WHAT IS IT
WHICH THESE WITNESS AGAINST THEE? BUT
JESUS HELD HIS PEACE. AND THE HIGH PRIEST
ANSWERED AND SAID UNTO HIM, I ADJURE
THEE BY THE LIVING GOD, THAT THOU TELL
US WHETHER THOU BE THE CHRIST, THE SON
OF GOD. JESUS SAITH UNTO HIM, THOU HAST
SAID: NEVERTHELESS I SAY UNTO YOU,
HEREAFTER SHALL YE SEE THE SON OF MAN
SITTING ON THE RIGHT HAND OF POWER, AND
COMING IN THE CLOUDS OF HEAVEN. THEN
THE HIGH PRIEST RENT HIS CLOTHES, SAYING,
HE HATH SPOKEN BLASPHEMY; WHAT
FURTHER NEED HAVE WE OF WITNESSES?
BEHOLD, NOW YE HAVE HEARD HIS BLAS-
PHEMY. WHAT THINK YE? THEY ANSWERED
AND SAID, HE IS GUILTY OF DEATH.

(Matt. 26:57-66) *(Figure 17)*

17. Christ before Caiaphas. (*Rembrandt drawing*)

Christ is accused of threatening to destroy the Holy Temple, the dwelling place of Yahweh's presence. That was in fact his hidden intention as revealed by the development of the Christian myth. He was thus a traitor to the old dispensation, the established collective container of religious values. This explains Caiaphas' attitude when he says in John 11:50, "It is expedient for us, that one man should die for the people, and that the whole nation perish not." The expressed fear of the priests was that, "If we let him thus alone, all men will believe on him: and the Romans shall come and take away both our place and our nation." (John 11:48) But even without the Romans Christ threatens Jewish orthodoxy. He is therefore on trial for heresy.

For a religious community heresy is spiritual treason, more

dangerous than treason to the state. We can measure the degree of psychic threat by the intensity of the defensive reaction evoked. By that measure, heresy for the true believer is the ultimate threat. It threatens the supreme *psychic* value and is therefore more dangerous than death which threatens only physical existence. It was this order of reaction that Christ constellated among the Jewish priests.

Heresy trials of course miss the whole point of the *reality of the psyche*. For the orthodox believer of any creed the psyche does not yet exist as an autonomous entity but only as a metaphysical hypostasis. It is this state of affairs that Christ is challenging. He admits that he is "the Christ, the Son of God" and this seals his physical doom. In the context this is not inflation. It is a witness to the reality of the transpersonal psyche as consciously manifested in the individual—the essential feature of individuation.

TRIAL BEFORE PILATE

THEN PILATE ENTERED INTO THE JUDGMENT HALL AGAIN, AND CALLED JESUS, AND SAID UNTO HIM, ART THOU THE KING OF THE JEWS? . . . JESUS ANSWERED, MY KINGDOM IS NOT OF THIS WORLD: IF MY KINGDOM WERE OF THIS WORLD, THEN WOULD MY SERVANTS FIGHT, THAT I SHOULD NOT BE DELIVERED TO THE JEWS: BUT NOW IS MY KINGDOM NOT FROM HENCE. PILATE THEREFORE SAID UNTO HIM, ART THOU A KING THEN? JESUS ANSWERED, THOU SAYEST THAT I AM A KING. TO THIS END WAS I BORN, AND FOR THIS CAUSE CAME I INTO THE WORLD, THAT I SHOULD BEAR WITNESS UNTO THE TRUTH. EVERY ONE THAT IS OF THE TRUTH HEARETH MY VOICE.   (John 18:33-37)

For Caiaphas the crucial question was, "Are you the son of God?" For Pilate it is, "Are you a king?" These are the religious and political versions of the same question. Psychologically, the question is, "Do you have an inner transpersonal authority which takes priority over collective religious and political authority?" To have such an authority makes one, symbolically speaking, a "son of God" and a "king."

9

Flagellation and Mocking

The divine process of change manifests itself to our human understanding . . . as punishment, torment, death, and transfiguration.[1]

1. Jung, "The Visions of Zosimos," *Alchemical Studies,* CW 13, par. 139.

18. Flagellation of Christ.
(*The Hours of Catherine of Cleves*)

THEN PILATE THEREFORE TOOK JESUS, AND
SCOURGED HIM.   (John 19:1) *(Figure 18)*

THEN THE SOLDIERS OF THE GOVERNOR TOOK
JESUS INTO THE COMMON HALL, AND GATH-
ERED UNTO HIM THE WHOLE BAND OF SOL-
DIERS. AND THEY STRIPPED HIM, AND PUT ON
HIM A SCARLET ROBE. AND WHEN THEY HAD
PLATTED A CROWN OF THORNS, THEY PUT IT
UPON HIS HEAD, AND A REED IN HIS RIGHT
HAND: AND THEY BOWED THE KNEE BEFORE
HIM, AND MOCKED HIM, SAYING, HAIL, KING
OF THE JEWS! AND THEY SPIT UPON HIM, AND
TOOK THE REED, AND SMOTE HIM ON THE
HEAD. AND AFTER THAT THEY HAD MOCKED
HIM, THEY TOOK THE ROBE OFF FROM HIM,
AND PUT HIS OWN RAIMENT ON HIM, AND LED
HIM AWAY TO CRUCIFY HIM.   (Matt. 27:27-31)
(Figure 19)

These events express utter degradation of the ego. Torture
and humiliation belong to the mortificatio phase of individuation.[2] "The experience of the self is always a defeat for the
ego."[3] The ego must be *relativized* to make room for the Self.
The totality of the Self brings with it the shadow, encounter
with which is always a painful humiliation. Only a day or two
earlier Christ had chastized the moneychangers in the temple.
(Figure 11) Now that chastisement is fed back on him many-
fold.

Christ's physical and psychological torture which culmi-

---

2. See Edinger, *Anatomy of the Psyche*, pp. 147ff.
3. Jung, *Mysterium Coniunctionis*, CW 14, par. 778.

19. Mocking of Christ. (*Rembrandt drawing*)

nates in the crucifixion has a parallel in the description of the "Suffering Servant of Yahweh" in Isaiah 53:

> He is despised and rejected of men; a man of sorrows, and acquainted with grief: and we hid as it were our faces from him; he was despised, and we esteemed him not. Surely he hath borne our griefs, and carried our sorrows: yet we did esteem him stricken, smitten of God, and afflicted. But he was wounded for our transgressions, he was bruised for our iniquities: the chastisement of our peace was upon him; and with his stripes we are healed. (verses 3-5)

> By his knowledge shall my righteous servant justify many; for he shall bear their iniquities. (verse 11)

The Suffering Servant of Yahweh can be understood as a personification of the redeeming nature of "consciousness of wholeness." It has nothing to do with meekly turning the other cheek, but rather refers to the fact that the individuated ego can endure the onslaught of the power principle without identifying with it, that is, without succumbing to either defensive violence or despair. The consequence is a gradual transformation of the collective psyche. "By his knowledge [consciousness] shall my righteous servant justify many." In this way, writes Jung, "was world-conquering Caesarism transformed into spiritual kingship."[4]

4. "The Development of Personality," *The Development of Personality,* CW 17, par. 309. The alchemists equated the torture of Christ with the transformation of the prima materia. See Jung, *Mysterium Coniunctionis,* CW 14, pars. 484ff.

10

Crucifixion

The reality of evil and its incompatibility with good cleave the opposites asunder and lead inexorably to the crucifixion and suspension of everything that lives. Since "the soul is by nature Christian" this result is bound to come as infallibly as it did in the life of Jesus: we all have to be "crucified with Christ," i.e., suspended in a moral suffering equivalent to veritable crucifixion.[1]

1. Jung, *Psychology and Alchemy*, CW 12, par. 24.

20. Crucifixion.
(*Early Spanish manuscript illumination*)

AND WHEN THEY WERE COME UNTO A PLACE
CALLED GOLGOTHA, THAT IS TO SAY, A PLACE
OF A SKULL, THEY GAVE HIM VINEGAR TO
DRINK MINGLED WITH GALL: AND WHEN HE
HAD TASTED THEREOF, HE WOULD NOT DRINK.
AND THEY CRUCIFIED HIM, AND PARTED HIS
GARMENTS, CASTING LOTS: THAT IT MIGHT BE
FULFILLED WHICH WAS SPOKEN BY THE
PROPHET, THEY PARTED MY GARMENTS
AMONG THEM, AND UPON MY VESTURE DID
THEY CAST LOTS. AND SITTING DOWN THEY
WATCHED HIM THERE; AND SET UP OVER HIS
HEAD HIS ACCUSATION WRITTEN, THIS IS
JESUS THE KING OF THE JEWS. THEN WERE
THERE TWO THIEVES CRUCIFIED WITH HIM,
ONE ON THE RIGHT HAND, AND ANOTHER ON
THE LEFT.　　　　　(Matt. 27:33-38) *(Figure 20)*

The crucifixion is *the* central image of the Western psyche.

The death of Christ on the cross is the central image in Christian art and the visual focus of Christian contemplation. The character of the image varied from one age to another reflecting the prevailing climate of religious thought and feeling. . . . The early Church avoided the subject. At the time when Christianity was a proscribed religion under the Romans the crucifixion was represented symbolically by the lamb of Christ juxtaposed with a cross. Even after the age of Constantine the Great, when Christians were allowed to practise their religion without interference, the cross itself was still represented without the figure of Christ. The image of the crucifixion as we know it is first found in the 6th Century but is rare until the Carolingian era when representations multiplied in ivories, metal work and manuscripts. At this period there are regularly found those other figures from the gospels which were to become a permanent feature of the crucifixion:

the Virgin Mary and St. John the Evangelist, the centurion
and the sponge bearer, the two thieves, the soldiers casting
lots. Also seen from this time on either side of the cross are
the symbolic sun and moon and the allegorical figures representing the Church and Synagogue; these latter features were
however to die out early in the Renaissance. For many centuries the west, under Byzantine influence, represented Christ
himself alive and open-eyed, a triumphant Savior wearing a
royal crown. In the 11th Century there appeared a new type,
the emaciated figure with its head fallen on one shoulder and,
later, wearing the crown of thorns. This version prevailed in
western art thereafter.[2]

Collective consciousness has thus altered its relation to this
image through the centuries. Initially it is expressed in an
archetypal, impersonal way with no indication of human suffering. The personal and human aspect increases up to the
Reformation, at which time Protestant iconoclasm removes
the figure of Christ from the cross entirely, signifying the
victory of rationalistic abstraction.

The crucifixion pictures the juxtaposition of opposites. It is
the moment of intersection between the human and the divine.
Ego and Self are superimposed. The human figure representing
the ego is nailed to the mandala-cross representing the Self.
Around the cross various pairs of opposites are constellated.
For instance, on either side of Christ two thieves are crucified.
One goes to heaven, the other to hell. This triple crucifixion
hints at the idea, only now thinkable, that Christ is uniting
himself with his opposite, the Antichrist:

> Although the attributes of Christ (consubstantiality with the
> Father, co-eternity, filiation, parthenogenesis, crucifixion,
> Lamb sacrificed between opposites, One divided into Many,
> etc.) undoubtedly mark him out as an embodiment of the self,
> looked at from the psychological angle he corresponds to only

2. James Hall, *Dictionary of Subjects and Symbols in Art*, p. 81.

one half of the archetype. The other half appears in the Antichrist. The latter is just as much a manifestation of the self, except that he consists of its dark aspect. Both are Christian symbols, and they have the same meaning as the image of the Saviour crucified between two thieves. This great symbol tells us that the progressive development and differentiation of consciousness leads to an ever more menacing awareness of the conflict and involves nothing less than a crucifixion of the ego, its agonizing suspension between irreconcilable opposites.[3]

Through the Christ crucified between the two thieves man gradually attained knowledge of his shadow and its duality. This duality had already been anticipated by the double meaning of the serpent. Just as the serpent stands for the power that heals as well as corrupts, so one of the thieves is destined upwards, the other downwards, and so likewise the shadow is on one side regrettable and reprehensible weakness, on the other side healthy instinctivity and the prerequisite for higher consciousness.[4]

Other pairs of opposites that gather around the cross include the lance-bearer and the sponge-bearer and even the sun and the moon. The crucifixion is clearly a coniunctio and thus manifests the phenomenology of that symbolism.[5] In ecclesiastical art there has been a definite tendency to turn the image of the crucifixion into a mandala. *(Figure 21)* In a remarkable figure of speech Augustine equates the crucifixion with the coniunctio:

> Like a bridegroom Christ went forth from his chamber, he went out with a presage of his nuptials into the field of the world. . . . He came to the marriage bed of the cross, and

3. Jung, *Aion,* CW 9ii, par. 79.
4. Ibid., par. 402. For the thieves as "redeemers of mankind," see Jung, "The Tavistock Lectures," *The Symbolic Life,* CW 18, par. 210.
5. See Edinger, *Anatomy of the Psyche,* pp. 211ff.

21. Crucifixion.
(*Cover of the Echternach Gospels*)

22. The Cross as a Tree.
(*Illumination of a Bible*)

there, in mounting it, he consummated his marriage. And when he perceived the sighs of the creature, he lovingly gave himself up to the torment in the place of his bride, . . . and he joined the woman to himself for ever.[6]

The product of the coniunctio is the Self represented by the Anthropos, the whole man. Adam symbolizes the first Anthropos[7] and Christ the second. This relationship is indicated by the legendary idea that the cross was a tree growing out of the grave of Adam. *(Figure 22)* This tree is said to have grown from a branch of the Tree of Life (in some versions, the Tree of Knowledge of good and evil).

Another image of the reborn Self appears in the sign of four letters (INRI) that is attached to the cross in conventional representations. *(Figure 23)* These letters stand for *Iesus Nazarenus Rex Iudaeorum*. In effect they constitute a new tetragrammaton. In the Old Testament Yahweh's name was never vocalized and appeared only as the four consonants, YHWH, *Yod Hē Waw Hē*.[8] Significantly, this is a quaternity which is at the same time a triad since one of the letters is duplicated—the "dilemma of the three and four."[9] The "new tetragrammaton" repeats this dilemma and demonstrates again the basic uniformities of the objective psyche.

6. Quoted in Jung, *Mysterium Coniunctionis,* par. 25, note 176, also par. 568.
7. Ibid., pars. 544ff.
8. Ibid., par. 619; see also Edinger, *The Bible and the Psyche,* p. 48.
9. "Three are here but where is the fourth?" is an important theme in alchemy. Psychologically it refers to the inordinate difficulty of assimilating the fourth, inferior function and thus achieving wholeness. Also, as Jung points out, "Four signifies the feminine, motherly, physical; three the masculine, fatherly, spiritual. Thus the uncertainty as to three or four amounts to a wavering between the spiritual and the physical—a striking example of how every human truth is a last truth but one." (*Psychology and Alchemy,* CW 12, par. 31)

23. Crucifixion.
(*Dürer woodcut*)

In early theology, the cross of Christ was considered to be the instrument that unified the universe. Paul says,

> He [Christ] is the peace between us and has made the two [Jew and Gentile] into one and broken down the barrier *[phragmos]* which used to keep them apart. . . . This was to create one single new man in himself out of the two of them and by restoring peace through the cross, to unite them both in a single Body and reconcile them with God. (Eph. 2:14-16, Jerusalem Bible)

Jean Daniélou comments,

> Paul's text in fact assumes a double *phragmos*. In the first place there is one that separates the two peoples . . . but there is also the *phragmos* separating the world below from the world above. This was a stock conception. . . . Among the Mandaeans . . . it represents the heavenly wall separating the world below from the Pleroma. The Apocryphal *Acts* also have it, in this case conceived as a wall of fire.
>
> In this view Christ restores unity in a twofold sense. He destroys both the vertical wall which separates the two peoples, and the horizontal one which separates man from God; and he does this by the Cross, which now seems to represent the double operation of Christ extending both vertically and horizontally to form a cross. These are also in a sense two crosses: the cross of separation which existed before the Coming of Christ, and the cross of unification which is the coming of Christ.[10]

The "two crosses" refer to the twofold aspect of mandala symbolism. In its simplest form, the cross within a circle, the mandala functions as the cross-hairs of a telescope—to order and discriminate different areas in the field of view. On the other hand it also unites all its embraces in a comprehensive

10. *The Theology of Jewish Christianity,* pp. 279f.

whole.[11] The Gnostics also speak of the twofold nature of the cross.

[The cross] . . . whom they call by a variety of names, has two faculties—the one of supporting, and the other of separating; and in so far as he supports and sustains, he is Stauros [Cross], while in so far as he divides and separates, he is Horos [Limit]. They then represent the Saviour as having indicated this twofold faculty: first, the sustaining power, when He said, "Whosoever doth not bear his cross (Stauros), and follow after me, cannot be my disciple;" [Luke 14:27] and again, "Taking up the cross, follow me;" [Matt. 10:21] but the separating power when He said, "I came not to send peace, but a sword." [Matt. 10:34][12]

And Jung states,

The apotropaic significance of the quaternity is borne out by Ezekiel 9:4, where the prophet, at the behest of the Lord, sets a cross on the foreheads of the righteous to protect them from punishment. It is evidently the sign of God, who himself has the attribute of quaternity. The cross is the mark of his protégés. As attributes of God and also symbols in their own right, the quaternity and the cross signify wholeness.[13]

11. The fact that the Christian cross emphasizes the vertical dimension at the expense of the horizontal indicates a bias in favor of spirit over matter.

12. Irenaeus, "Against Heresies," I, 3, 5, *The Ante-Nicene Fathers,* vol. 1, p. 320.

13. "The Philosophical Tree," *Alchemical Studies,* CW 13, par. 363.

11

Lamentation and Entombment

The God-image in man was not destroyed by the Fall but was only damaged and corrupted ("deformed"), and can be restored through God's grace. The scope of the integration is suggested by the descensus ad inferos, *the descent of Christ's soul to hell, its work of redemption embracing even the dead. The psychological equivalent of this is the integration of the collective unconscious which forms an essential part of the individuation process.*[1]

1. Jung, *Aion*, CW 9ii, par. 72.

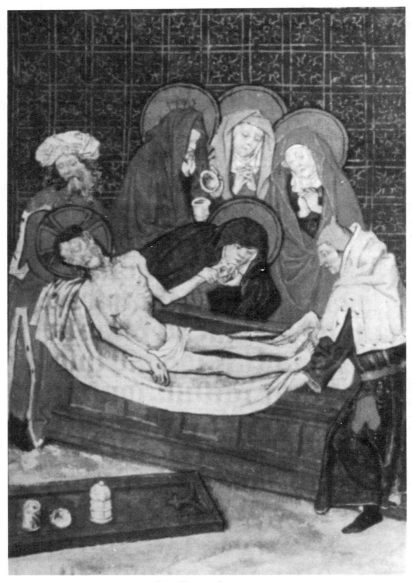

24. Entombment.
(*The Hours of Catherine of Cleves*)

AND WHEN JOSEPH HAD TAKEN THE BODY, HE
WRAPPED IT IN A CLEAN LINEN CLOTH, AND
LAID IT IN HIS OWN NEW TOMB, WHICH HE HAD
HEWN OUT IN THE ROCK: AND HE ROLLED A
GREAT STONE TO THE DOOR OF THE SEPUL-
CHRE, AND DEPARTED. AND THERE WAS MARY
MAGDALENE, AND THE OTHER MARY, SITTING
OVER AGAINST THE SEPULCHRE.

(Matt. 27:59-61) *(Figure 24)*

Although the gospels are silent on the subject, in devotional
art the death of Christ on the cross is followed by Mary's
lamentation (Pièta) over the dead body. This image of the
Mater Dolorosa has a number of parallels in mythology and
ancient Near Eastern religion, notably, Isis' lamentation for
Osiris. A mother's love for her firstborn is perhaps the most
powerful instinctual attachment of the human psyche. To lose
the object of such intense possessive love challenges the very
foundation of desirousness, the primordial psyche itself. The
archetypal image of the Great Mother's lamentation for her
dead son thus signifies *natural libido deprived of its object.*
This corresponds to the necessary mortificatio phase of the
alchemical process of transformation.[2] Lamentation for the
dead Christ has an additional implication for modern man:
Mary represents humanity mourning its loss of the eternal
images, wailing "a threnody for the lost god."[3]

According to apocryphal accounts, between Good Friday
and Easter Sunday Christ descended into hell and rescued
ancient worthies—the so-called "harrowing of hell." *(Figure
25)*

The Christian tenet that after his death Christ descended into
hell has no very clear scriptural basis, but the concept appealed

2. See Edinger, *Anatomy of the Psyche,* chap. 6.
3. Jung, *Mysterium Coniunctionis,* CW 14, par. 510.

strongly to the early Church, and it first became an article of faith in the 4th cent. The god or hero who descends to the lower regions to fetch the dead back to the upper world is well-known in classical mythology, and may have been the seed out of which the Christian idea grew. As early as the 2nd cent. there existed a body of writing containing descriptions of Christ's descent, how he overcame Satan and liberated the souls of the Old Testament saints. It was taught that because they lived and died in an era that was without benefit of the Christian sacraments they were relegated to a lower place until such time as Christ should come to redeem them. The story is first told as a continuous narrative in the apocryphal Gospel of Nicodemus (perhaps 5th cent.) where we read that "the gates of brass were broken in pieces . . . and all the dead that were bound were loosed from their chains . . . and the King of glory entered in." After Satan had been bound in irons, "the Saviour blessed Adam upon his forehead with the sign of the cross, and so did he also unto all the patriarchs and prophets and martyrs and forefathers. And he took them and leaped up out of hell." The early Fathers of the Church who speculated about the matter concluded that the precise region was not in hell itself but on its border, or Limbo (Lat. *limbus,* a hem). The subject enjoyed great popularity in medieval drama and literature. In Dante's *Inferno* (canto 4) Limbo forms the first Circle of Hell and its inhabitants include the virtuous pagans, poets, philosophers and heroes of classical antiquity. In medieval art the subject formed one of the scenes in the cycle of Christ's Passion. It continued to be represented through the Renaissance but is seldom found after the 16th cent.[4]

This symbolic image, which has classical parallels in the myths of Odysseus, Orpheus, Alcestis and Heracles, is of the greatest importance to depth psychology. It represents the ego's deliberate descent into the unconscious, the *nekyia.* The

4. James Hall, *Dictionary of Subjects and Symbols in Art,* p. 100.

25. Descent into Limbo.
(*The Grandes Heures of Jean, Duke of Berry*)

light of the ego is temporarily extinguished in the upper world and is carried into the lower world where it rescues worthy contents of the unconscious and even conquers Death itself. The latter is perhaps an allusion to the idea that the *nekyia* "eternalizes" the ego, that is, connects it with the infinite.[5]

The "world of the dead" represents the unconscious, especially the collective unconscious. Thus during his confrontation with the collective unconscious Jung had dreams and visions of visiting "the dead" and bringing them back to life.[6] About these experiences, he says,

> From that time on, the dead have become ever more distinct for me as the voices of the Unanswered, Unresolved, and Unredeemed. . . . These conversations with the dead formed a kind of prelude to what I had to communicate to the world about the unconscious. . . . It was then that I ceased to belong to myself alone, ceased to have the right to do so. From then on, my life belonged to the generality.[7]

Belonging to the "generality" corresponds to being connected with the "infinite." The ego is relativized. It acknowledges a supraordinate authority and experiences itself *sub specie aeternitatis.*

---

5. "The decisive question for man is: Is he related to something infinite or not?" (Jung, *Memories, Dreams, Reflections,* p. 325)
6. See Jung's discussion of his "Seven Sermons to the Dead," *Memories, Dreams, Reflections,* pp. 191f, and (in paperback edition only) appendix 5, pp. 378ff; see also the dream Jung reports on pp. 172f.
7. Ibid., pp. 191f.

12

Resurrection and Ascension

*I only know—and here I am expressing
what countless other people know—that
the present is a time of God's death and
disappearance. The myth says he was
not to be found where his body was laid.
"Body" means the outward, visible
form, the erstwhile but ephemeral setting for the highest value. The myth
further says that the value rose again in
a miraculous manner, transformed. It
looks like a miracle, for, when a value
disappears, it always seems to be lost
irretrievably. So it is quite unexpected
that it should come back. The three
days' descent into hell during death
describes the sinking of the vanished
value into the unconscious, where, by
conquering the power of darkness, it
establishes a new order, and then rises
up to heaven again, that is, attains
supreme clarity of consciousness. The
fact that only a few people see the Risen
One means that no small difficulties
stand in the way of finding and recognizing the transformed value.*[1]

1. Jung, "Psychology and Religion," *Psychology and Religion*, CW 11,
   par. 149.

113

26. Resurrection.
(*The Hours of Catherine of Cleves*)

RESURRECTION

NOW UPON THE FIRST DAY OF THE WEEK, VERY
EARLY IN THE MORNING, THEY CAME UNTO
THE SEPULCHRE, BRINGING THE SPICES WHICH
THEY HAD PREPARED, AND CERTAIN OTHERS
WITH THEM. AND THEY FOUND THE STONE
ROLLED AWAY FROM THE SEPULCHRE. AND
THEY ENTERED IN, AND FOUND NOT THE BODY
OF THE LORD JESUS. AND IT CAME TO PASS, AS
THEY WERE MUCH PERPLEXED THEREABOUT,
BEHOLD, TWO MEN STOOD BY THEM IN SHIN-
ING GARMENTS: AND AS THEY WERE AFRAID,
AND BOWED DOWN THEIR FACES TO THE
EARTH, THEY SAID UNTO THEM, WHY SEEK YE
THE LIVING AMONG THE DEAD? HE IS NOT
HERE, BUT IS RISEN.   (Luke 24:1-6) *(Figure 26)*

After the discovery of the empty tomb there are several
accounts of encounter with the risen Christ. Mary Magdalene
is the first to meet him but mistakes him for the gardener.
(John 20:11-17) He appeared to the eleven disciples on a
mountain in Galilee "but some doubted." (Matt. 28:16,17)
Two disciples meet him on the road to Emmaus, "But their
eyes were holden that they should not know him." (Luke
24:13-16) He appeared again to the eleven in Luke 24:36f,
"But they were terrified and affrighted, and supposed that
they had seen a spirit." And finally he appeared to the disciples
fishing in the sea of Tiberias. "Jesus stood on the shore: but
the disciples knew not that it was Jesus." (John 21:4)

The fact that the risen Christ is not recognized at first, even
by his intimate companions, "means that no small difficulties
stand in the way of finding and recognizing the transformed

value."[2] These difficulties concern the transition from Christ to the Holy Ghost, that is, the transition from commitment to a concrete, external value to the inner autonomous psyche.

Christ's resurrection has its parallel in the reconstitution of the dismember/ed[3] body of Osiris by Isis. This was accomplished by anointing it, thus inaugurating the Egyptian embalming process which transforms the deceased into an "immortal body." This process takes forty days. (Gen. 50:3) "'Forty' is a prefiguration of the [alchemical] opus,"[4] and corresponds to the length of time between Christ's resurrection and ascension. The death and rebirth of Christ and Osiris correspond to the death and rebirth sequence in the individuation process. Following the mortificatio (nigredo) comes the dawn of the reborn sun (rubedo). This archetypal event is mirrored externally by the death and rebirth of the vegetation spirit each winter and spring. Out of blackness comes the green. Jung writes,

> The state of imperfect transformation, merely hoped for and waited for, does not seem to be one of torment only, but of positive, if hidden, happiness. It is the state of someone who, in his wanderings among the mazes of his psychic transformation, comes upon a secret happiness which reconciles him to his apparent loneliness. In communing with himself he finds not deadly boredom and melancholy but an inner partner; more than that, a relationship that seems like the happiness of a secret love, or like a hidden springtime, when the green seed sprouts from the barren earth, holding out the promise of future harvests. It is the alchemical *benedicta viriditas,* the

2. Ibid.

3. To record a piece of synchronicity: On June 3, 1981, while writing this word in the original draft, I was interrupted by a telephone call which informed me of the death of my son, Ronald, a young man fated to live out this archetype.

4. Jung, *Mysterium Coniunctionis,* CW 14, par. 77, note 215.

blessed greenness, signifying on the one hand the "leprosy of the metals" (verdigris), but on the other the secret immanence of the divine spirit of life in all things.[5]

In the remarkable fifteenth chapter of I Corinthians, Paul gives us a description of the resurrection archetype:

Someone may ask, "How are dead people raised, and what sort of body do they have when they come back?" They are stupid questions. Whatever you sow in the ground has to die before it is given new life and the thing that you sow is not what is going to come; you sow a bare grain, say of wheat or something like that, and then God gives it the sort of body that he has chosen: each sort of seed gets its own sort of body.

Everything that is flesh is not the same flesh: there is human flesh, animals' flesh, the flesh of birds and the flesh of fish. Then there are heavenly bodies and there are earthly bodies; but the heavenly bodies have a beauty of their own and the earthly bodies a different one. The sun has its brightness, the moon a different brightness, and the stars a different brightness, and the stars differ from each other in brightness. It is the same with the resurrection of the dead: the thing that is sown is perishable but what is raised is imperishable; the thing that is sown is contemptible but what is raised is glorious; the thing that is sown is weak but what is raised is powerful; when it is sown it embodies the soul, when it is raised it embodies the spirit.

If the soul has its own embodiment, so does the spirit have its own embodiment. The first *man,* Adam, as scripture says, *became a living soul,* but the last Adam has become a life-giving spirit. That is, first the one with the soul, not the spirit, and after that, the one with the spirit. The first man, being from the earth, is earthly by nature; the second man is from heaven. As this earthly man was, so are we on earth; and as

5. Ibid., par. 623. Jung also notes that "green is the colour of the Holy Ghost." (Ibid., par. 395)

the heavenly man is, so are we in heaven. And we, who have been modelled on the earthly man, will be modelled on the heavenly man.

Or else, brothers, put it this way: flesh and blood cannot inherit the kingdom of God: and the perishable cannot inherit what lasts for ever. I will tell you something that has been secret: that we are not all going to die, but we shall all be changed. This will be instantaneous, in the twinkling of an eye, when the last trumpet sounds. It will sound, and the dead will be raised, imperishable, and we shall be changed as well, because our present perishable nature must put on imperishability and this mortal nature must put on immorality. (verses 35-53, Jerusalem Bible)

Jung states the same idea in modern terms:

The utter failure came at the Crucifixion in the tragic words, "My God, my God, why hast thou forsaken me?" If you want to understand the full tragedy of those words you must realize what they meant: Christ saw that his whole life, devoted to the truth according to his best conviction, had been a terrible illusion. He had lived it to the full absolutely sincerely, he had made his honest experiment, but it was nevertheless a compensation. On the cross his mission deserted him. But *because he had lived so fully and devotedly he won through to the Resurrection body.*[6]

Jung's "Resurrection body" corresponds to Paul's "celestial body" (1 Cor. 15:40). What they refer to is beyond our conscious grasp. My own hypothesis is that they refer to the ultimate goal of individuation—the transformation of ego into archetype.[7]

The death and resurrection of Christ is an archetype which lives itself out not only in the individual but also in the collec-

6. *C.G. Jung Speaking,* pp. 97f, italics mine.
7. See Edinger, *The Creation of Consciousness,* pp. 23ff.

tive psyche. There are certain periods in history when the collective God-image undergoes death and rebirth. Such is now the case. The twentieth century is the Holy Saturday of history.

> When Nietzsche said "God is dead," he uttered a truth which is valid for the greater part of Europe. People were influenced by it not because he said so, but because it stated a widespread psychological fact. The consequences were not long delayed: after the fog of -isms, the catastrophe.[8]

> We are living in what the Greeks called the *kairos*—the right moment—for a "metamorphosis of the gods," of the fundamental principles and symbols. This peculiarity of our time . . . is the expression of the unconscious man within us who is changing.[9]

ASCENSION

The resurrection is actually the first term in a threefold sequence: resurrection, ascent, descent (Pentecost). The ascension is described in Acts 1:8-11. Jesus says to his disciples:

> YE SHALL RECEIVE POWER, AFTER THAT THE
> HOLY GHOST IS COME UPON YOU: AND YE
> SHALL BE WITNESSES UNTO ME BOTH IN
> JERUSALEM, AND IN ALL JUDAEA, AND IN
> SAMARIA AND UNTO THE UTTERMOST PART OF
> THE EARTH. AND WHEN HE HAD SPOKEN THESE
> THINGS, WHILE THEY BEHELD, HE WAS TAKEN
> UP; AND A CLOUD RECEIVED HIM OUT OF THEIR

8. Jung, "Psychology and Religion," *Psychology and Religion*, CW 11, par. 145.
9. Jung, "The Undiscovered Self," *Civilization in Transition*, CW 10, par. 585.

SIGHT. AND WHILE THEY LOOKED STEDFASTLY TOWARD HEAVEN AS HE WENT UP, BEHOLD, TWO MEN STOOD BY THEM IN WHITE APPAREL; WHICH ALSO SAID, YE MEN OF GALILEE, WHY STAND YE GAZING UP INTO HEAVEN? THIS SAME JESUS, WHICH IS TAKEN UP FROM YOU INTO HEAVEN, SHALL SO COME IN LIKE MANNER AS YE HAVE SEEN HIM GO INTO HEAVEN.

(Figure 27)

The last remark is usually understood to refer to the *parousia*,[10] however it could equally well refer to the coming of the Holy Ghost at Pentecost, especially since Christ is speaking of the Holy Ghost's coming at the beginning of the passage. Christ is God-man and therefore carrier of a paradox. Considered as God he originated in heaven, descended to earth in his incarnation and returned to heaven in the Ascension. However, considered as man, he originated on earth, ascended to heaven and returned to earth as the Holy Ghost (or Paraclete). The latter sequence of ascent followed by descent corresponds to alchemical symbolism. The *Emerald Tablet of Hermes,* a recipe for creating the Philosophers' Stone, includes these words: "It ascends from the earth to the heaven, and descends again to the earth, and receives the power of the above and below."[11] Commenting on this passage Jung writes,

> [For the alchemist] . . . it is not a question of a one-way ascent to heaven, but, in contrast to the route followed by the Christian Redeemer, who comes from above to below and from there returns to the above, the *filius macrocosmi* starts from below, ascends on high, and, with the powers of Above and Below united in himself, returns to earth again. He carries

10. The Second Coming of Christ.
11. See Edinger, *Anatomy of the Psyche,* pp. 142 and 231.

27. Ascension.
(*Rembrandt painting*)

out the reverse movement and thereby manifests a nature contrary to that of Christ and the Gnostic Redeemers.[12]

The question: Does the redeemer originate on earth or heaven? suggests the psychological question: Does individuation originate from the ego or the Self? This confronts us with the ego-Self paradox.

> The self, like the unconscious, is an *a priori* existent out of which the ego evolves. It is, so to speak, an unconscious prefiguration of the ego. It is not I who create myself, rather I happen to myself. . . . [However] psychology must reckon with the fact that despite the causal nexus man does enjoy a feeling of freedom, which is identical with autonomy of consciousness. . . . The existence of ego consciousness has meaning only if it is free and autonomous. By stating these facts we have, it is true, established an antimony, but we have at the same time given a picture of things as they are. . . . In reality both are always present: the supremacy of the self and the hybris of consciousness.[13]

12. "The Spirit Mercurius," *Alchemical Studies,* CW 13, par. 280.

13. Jung, "Transformation Symbolism in the Mass," *Psychology and Religion,* CW 11, par. 391. The same essay in *The Mysteries: Papers from the Eranos Yearbooks* adds these sentences: "If ego consciousness follows its own road exclusively, it is trying to become like a god or a superman. But exclusive recognition of its dependence only leads to a childish fatalism and to a world-negating and misanthropic spiritual arrogance." (P. 324)

13

Pentecost

*Origen said of the Three Persons, that
the Father is the greatest and the Holy
Spirit the least. This is true inasmuch as
the Father by descending from the cosmic immensity became the least by
incarnating himself within the narrow
bounds of the human soul. . . .*

*The "littleness" of the Holy Spirit
stems from the fact that God's pneuma
dissolves into the form of little flames,
remaining none the less intact and
whole. His dwelling in a certain number
of human individuals and their transformation into* huiōi tou theou[1] *signifies a
very important step forward beyond
"Christocentrism." . . . On the level of
the Son there is no answer to the question of good and evil; there is only an
incurable separation of the opposites. . . . It seems to me to be the Holy
Spirit's task and charge to reconcile and
reunite the opposites in the human individual through a special development of
the human soul.*[2]

1. Sons of God.
2. Jung, "Letter to Père Lachat," *The Symbolic Life*, CW 18, pars. 1552f.

28. Pentecost.
(*The Très Riches Heures of Jean, Duke of Berry*)

AND WHEN THE DAY OF PENTECOST WAS
FULLY COME, THEY WERE ALL WITH ONE
ACCORD IN ONE PLACE. AND SUDDENLY THERE
CAME A SOUND FROM HEAVEN AS OF A RUSH-
ING MIGHTY WIND, AND IT FILLED ALL THE
HOUSE WHERE THEY WERE SITTING. AND
THERE APPEARED UNTO THEM CLOVEN
TONGUES LIKE AS OF FIRE, AND IT SAT UPON
EACH OF THEM. AND THEY WERE ALL FILLED
WITH THE HOLY GHOST, AND BEGAN TO SPEAK
WITH OTHER TONGUES, AS THE SPIRIT GAVE
THEM UTTERANCE. AND THERE WERE DWELL-
ING AT JERUSALEM JEWS, DEVOUT MEN, OUT
OF EVERY NATION UNDER HEAVEN. NOW
WHEN THIS WAS NOISED ABROAD, THE MUL-
TITUDE CAME TOGETHER, AND WERE CON-
FOUNDED, BECAUSE THAT EVERY MAN HEARD
THEM SPEAK IN HIS OWN LANGUAGE. AND
THEY WERE ALL AMAZED AND MARVELLED,
SAYING ONE TO ANOTHER, BEHOLD, ARE NOT
ALL THESE WHICH SPEAK GALILAEANS? AND
HOW HEAR WE EVERY MAN IN OUR OWN
TONGUE, WHEREIN WE WERE BORN? PARTH-
IANS AND MEDES, AND ELAMITES, AND THE
DWELLERS IN MESOPOTAMIA, AND IN JUDAEA,
AND CAPPADOCIA, IN PONTUS, AND ASIA,
PHRYGIA, AND PAMPHYLIA, IN EGYPT, AND IN
THE PARTS OF LIBYA ABOUT CYRENE, AND
STRANGERS OF ROME, JEWS AND PROSELYTES,
CRETES AND ARABIANS, WE DO HEAR THEM
SPEAK IN OUR TONGUES THE WONDERFUL
WORKS OF GOD. AND THEY WERE ALL
AMAZED, AND WERE IN DOUBT, SAYING ONE
TO ANOTHER, WHAT MEANETH THIS? OTHERS
MOCKING SAID, THESE MEN ARE FULL OF NEW
WINE.   (Acts 2:1-13) *(Figure 28)*

With Pentecost the incarnation cycle comes full circle. It began with the descent of the Holy Spirit at the Annunciation. After going through the cycle of events that make up the life of Christ the Holy Spirit returned in the Ascension to its origin. Now it descends again and a new cycle begins, as shown in the diagram opposite.

During Christ's life the Holy Spirit manifested itself in him. He was conceived by the Holy Spirit and anointed with it at his baptism. When he ascended he took the Holy Spirit with him, so to speak, leaving the earth deprived of the transcendent factor. He predicted however that after he left the Holy Spirit would return.

> It is for your own good that I am going
> because unless I go
> the Advocate [Paraclete] will not come to you;
> but if I do go,
> I will send him to you. (John 16:7, Jerusalem Bible)

> I shall ask the Father,
> and he will give you another Advocate [Paraclete]
> to be with you for ever,
> that Spirit of truth
> whom the world can never receive
> since it neither sees nor knows him;
> but you know him,
> because he is with you, he is in you.
> I will not leave you orphans;
> I will come back to you.
> In a short time the world will no longer see me;
> but you will see me,
> because I live and you will live.
> On that day
> you will understand that I am in my Father
> and you in me and I in you.
>
> (John 14:16-20, Jerusalem Bible)

Christ, as a particular concrete manifestation of the Holy

THE INCARNATION CYCLE

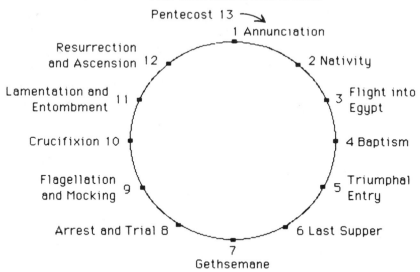

Spirit, must die in order for the disciples to develop an *individual* relation to the Holy Spirit, that is, the projection must be withdrawn. This is the "very important step forward beyond 'Christocentrism.'"[3] This step did not take place at the death of Christ. The individual did not become the vessel for the Holy Spirit. Instead, a collective container, the Church, emerged as vessel of the Holy Ghost.

Pentecost is considered to be the birthday of the Church. According to Pope Leo,

> the Church which, already conceived, came forth from the very side of the Second Adam, when he was, as it were, sleeping upon the cross, first showed herself in a marvellous manner before the eyes of men on the great day of Pentecost.[4]

3. Ibid., par. 1553.
4. Quoted in George D. Smith, ed., *The Teaching of the Catholic Church,* vol. 1, p. 159.

The central presence of the Virgin Mary, in the conventional representations of Pentecost, which has no scriptural basis, is considered to stand for the Church. The development of a community of believers serves to protect the individual from the onslaught of a private encounter with the *numinosum*. Thus the Church does not expect and dare not countenance any new or individual revelations. According to its teaching,

> the Holy Ghost's mission to the Church is to ensure the safe custody of an unchanging revelation . . . . [for] after the death of the Apostles no new economy or new revelation was to be expected, and, further, that there never has been nor will be any objective increase in revealed truth.[5]

The Church as the "body of Christ" had its Annunciation and conception at Pentecost. It was then fated to repeat the sequence of events that constitute the incarnation cycle concluding in its own death and ascension. This prospect is apparently not unknown among theologians but it is projected onto the "last day." The Catholic theologian Hugo Rahner explained it to Jung this way:

> The fundamental idea of the theologians is always this: the earthly fate of the Church as the body of Christ is modelled on the earthly fate of Christ himself. That is to say the Church, in the course of her history, moves towards a death . . . until the last day when, after fulfilling her earthly task, she becomes "unnecessary" and "dies," as indicated in Psalm 71:7: "until the moon shall fail." These ideas were expressed in the symbolism of Luna as the Church. Just as the *kenosis* of Christ was fulfilled in death . . . even so it is with the parallel *kenosis* of Ecclesia-Luna.[6]

If the death of the Church can be postponed to the "last day," then, as Jung says,

---

5. Ibid.
6. Jung, *Mysterium Coniunctionis*, CW 14, par. 28, note 194.

The man who is not particularly bold . . . will . . . thank God that the Holy Spirit does not concern himself with us over-much. One feels much safer under the shadow of the Church, which serves as a fortress to protect us against God and his Spirit. It is very comforting to be assured by the Catholic Church that it "possesses" the Spirit, who assists regularly at its rites. Then one knows that he is well chained up.[7]

If, however, the Church is destined to complete its incarnation cycle some time before the "last day," then we can expect the cycle to be circled once again, perhaps this time with the individual as the vessel of the Holy Spirit. This brings us to Jung's idea of continuing incarnation:

> The continuing, direct operation of the Holy Ghost on those who are called to be God's children implies, in fact, a broadening process of incarnation. Christ, the son begotten by God, is the first-born who is succeeded by an ever-increasing number of younger brothers and sisters. These are, however, neither begotten by the Holy Ghost nor born of a virgin. . . . Their lowly origin (possibly from the mammals) does not prevent them from entering into a close kinship with God as their father and Christ as their brother.[8]

> [There is a] . . . continued and progressive divine incarnation. Thus man is received and integrated into the divine drama. He seems destined to play a decisive part in it; that is why he must receive the Holy Spirit. I look upon the receiving of the Holy Spirit as a highly revolutionary fact which cannot take place until the ambivalent nature of the Father is recognized. If God is the *summum bonum*, the incarnation makes no sense, for a good god could never produce such hate and anger that his only son had to be sacrificed to appease it. A Midrash says that the Shofar is still sounded on the Day of Atonement to remind YHWH of his act of injustice towards Abraham (by

7. "Letter to Père Lachat," *The Symbolic Life,* CW 18, par. 1534.
8. "Answer to Job," *Psychology and Religion,* CW 11, par. 658.

compelling him to slay Isaac) and to prevent him from repeat-
ing it. A conscientious clarification of the idea of God would
have consequences as upsetting as they are necessary. They
would be indispensable for an interior development of the
trinitarian drama and of the role of the Holy Spirit. The Spirit
is destined to be incarnate in man or to choose him as a tran-
sitory dwelling-place. "Non habet nomen proprium," says St.
Thomas; because he will receive the name of man. That is
why he must not be identified with Christ. We cannot receive
the Holy Spirit unless we have accepted our own individual
life as Christ accepted his. Thus we become the "sons of god"
fated to experience the conflict of the divine opposites, represented by the crucifixion.[9]

9. "Letter to Père Lachat," *The Symbolic Life,* CW 18, par. 1551.

14

Assumption and Coronation of Mary

> *The dogmatization of the* Assumptio
> Mariae *points to the* hieros gamos *in the
> pleroma, and this in turn implies . . .
> the future birth of the divine child, who,
> in accordance with the divine trend
> towards incarnation, will choose as his
> birthplace the empirical man. The
> metaphysical process is known to the
> psychology of the unconscious as the
> individuation process.*[1]

The Assumption of Mary lies outside the incarnation cycle
and, perhaps for that reason, has no scriptural basis. It is a
product of legend and spontaneous collective belief.

For many centuries celebrated as a Church festival, the
Assumption was in 1950 declared an article of faith by Pius
XII. There is no scriptural foundation for the belief which
rests on the apocryphal literature of the 3rd and 4th cents.,
and the Tradition of the Catholic Church. It forms the continu-
ation of the narrative of the DEATH OF THE VIRGIN. The
13th cent., a period when the cult of the Virgin was ardently
fostered, saw the appearance of the *Golden Legend,* a popular
source-book for artists, in which the apocryphal story was
retold. As the apostles were sitting by the Virgin's tomb on
the third day, Christ appeared to them with St. Michael who
brought with him the Virgin's soul. "And anon the soul came
again to the body of Mary, and issued gloriously out of the
tomb, and thus was received in the heavenly chamber, and a

1. Jung, "Answer to Job," *Psychology and Religion,* CW 11, par. 755.

29. Coronation of the Virgin.
(*The Très Riches Heures of Jean, Duke of Berry*)

great company of angels with her." The Assumption was first widely represented in 13th cent. Gothic sculpture, especially in the portals of churches dedicated to the Virgin, and was to remain an important devotional theme in religious art.[2]

The Coronation in its most usual form shows the Virgin seated beside Christ who is in the act of placing a crown on her head. She may alternatively be kneeling before him. Or she may be crowned by God the Father.[3] *(Figure 29)*

For our purposes the Assumption of Mary can be considered as the comprehensive, summarizing image that expresses the fruit of the incarnation cycle taken as a whole, namely, the coniunctio. In the same decade that Jung was announcing the empirical discovery of the coniunctio archetype,[4] the Pope announced the dogmatization of the Assumption of Mary (1950)—which event Jung considers to be "the most important religious event since the Reformation."[5] This remarkable piece of historical synchronicity underscores the fact that the coniunctio is *the* relevant symbol for modern man.

The nuptial union in the *thalamus* (bridal-chamber) signifies the *hieros gamos,* and this in turn is the first step towards incarnation, towards the birth of the saviour who, since antiquity, was thought of as the *filius solis et lunae,* the *filius sapientiae,* and the equivalent of Christ. When, therefore, a longing for the exaltation of the Mother of God passes through the people, this tendency, if thought to its logical conclusion, means the desire for the birth of a saviour, a peacemaker, a "mediator pacem faciens inter inimicos."[6] Although he is

2. James Hall, *Dictionary of Subjects and Symbols in Art,* p. 34.
3. Ibid., p. 76.
4. In "The Psychology of the Transference" (1946), *The Practice of Psychotherapy,* CW 16, and *Mysterium Coniunctionis* (1955), CW 14.
5. "Answer to Job," *Psychology and Religion,* CW 11, par. 752.
6. "A mediator making peace between enemies."

already born in the pleroma, his birth in time can only be accomplished when it is perceived, recognized, and declared by man.[7]

Elsewhere Jung points out that the Assumption of Mary transforms the Trinity of Christian dogma into a quaternity, "thus making a dogmatic reality of those medieval representations of the quaternity which are constructed on the following pattern":[8]

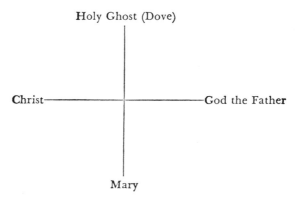

Holy Ghost (Dove)

Christ————————————————God the Father

Mary

The Assumption of Mary was prominent in alchemical symbolism which anticipated the relevance of this image for the modern mind. The symbolism is expressed in condensed form in a picture from Reusner's *Pandora* (1588). *(Figure 30)*

The picture is titled, "A Mirror Image of the Holy Trinity." It represents the coronation of Mary who takes her place with the Holy Trinity. This event in heaven is mirrored on earth by a strange image representing the extraction of the spirit Mercurius from the *prima materia*. The four corners are occupied by the symbols of the four evangelists, the typical figures which constitute the Christian quaternity.

7. Jung, "Answer to Job," *Psychology and Religion,* CW 11, par. 748.
8. *Mysterium Coniunctionis,* CW 14, par. 237.

In the lower portion of the picture is a lump of matter out of which a monstrous creature is being pulled by a crowned and haloed figure. The monster has a haloed human head, human legs, snakes for arms, and wings on the body of a fish. About this picture Jung writes,

30. Coronation of the Virgin and the Extraction of Mercurius.
(*Alchemical drawing*)

The taking up of the body had long been emphasized as an historical and material event, and the alchemists could therefore make use of the representations of the Assumption in describing the glorification of matter in the opus. The illustration of this process in Reusner's *Pandora* shows, underneath the coronation scene, a kind of shield between the emblems of Matthew and Luke, on which is depicted the extraction of Mercurius from the prima materia. The extracted spirit appears in monstrous form: the head is surrounded by a halo, and reminds us of the traditional head of Christ, but the arms are snakes and the lower half of the body resembles a stylized fish's tail. This is without doubt the *anima mundi* who has been freed from the shackles of matter, the *filius macrocosmi* or Mercurius-Anthropos, who, because of his double nature, is not only spiritual and physical but unites in himself the morally highest and lowest. The illustration in *Pandora* points to the great secret which the alchemists dimly felt was implicit in the Assumption. The proverbial darkness of sublunary matter has always been associated with the "prince of this world," the devil. He is the metaphysical figure who is excluded from the Trinity but who, as the counterpart of Christ, is the *sine qua non* of the drama of redemption. His equivalent in alchemy is the dark side of Mercurius duplex and . . . the active sulphur. He also conceals himself in the poisonous dragon, the preliminary, chthonic form of the *lapis aethereus*.[9]

In heaven the Trinity is being transformed into a quaternity by the addition of Mary who represents the principle of materiality. On earth, crude matter is being transformed by the extraction (bringing to consciousness) of the autonomous spirit hidden within it. Earth and egohood have gained a place in heaven and simultaneously matter is found to have a spiritual dimension.

The extraction process begins with a lump of crude matter.

9. Ibid., par. 238.

This can be understood as signifying all the problematical realities of incarnated existence.

> The slings and arrows of outrageous fortune,/ . . . The heartache and the thousand natural shocks/That flesh is heir to. . . ./ . . . . the whips and scorns of time,/The oppressor's wrong, the proud man's contumely,/The pangs of disprized love, the law's delay,/The insolence of office, and the spurns/ That patient merit of the unworthy takes,/. . . To grunt and sweat under a weary life. . . .[10]

Out of the lump, a bizarre creature is being pulled by a crowned and haloed man. This man can be considered as the "Christified" ego, that is, the ego operating under the aegis of the Self. In heaven the principle of materiality is being glorified. On earth the task of realizing that glorification is taking place through the redemption and transformation of concrete, personal existence by means of the individuating ego, that is, an ego that is carrying the process of continuing incarnation.

It is shocking that "the *anima mundi* who has been freed from the shackles of matter" should be a monstrosity. This alludes to the fact that the living experience of the Self is an aberration, a joining of opposites that appalls the ego and exposes it to anguish, demoralization and violation of all "reasonable" considerations. And yet the same event viewed from above is a coronation, demonstrating once again the reciprocal and compensatory relation between the ego and the unconscious.

The goal of the incarnation cycle, like the goal of individuation, is the coniunctio. The time has come for the psychic opposites—heaven and earth, male and female, spirit and nature, good and evil—which have long been torn asunder in the Western psyche, to be reconciled.

10. William Shakespeare, *Hamlet,* act 3, scene 1.

Bibliography

Adler, Gerhard. "Aspects of Jung's Personality and Work." *Psychological Perspectives,* Spring 1975.

The Ante-Nicene Fathers. 10 vols. Ed. Alexander Roberts and James Donaldson. Grand Rapids, Mich.: Eerdmans, 1977.

Daniélou, Jean. *The Theology of Jewish Christianity.* Trans. John A. Baker. Philadelphia: The Westminster Press, 1978.

Donne, John. "Holy Sonnets." *The Major Metaphysical Poets of the Seventeenth Century.* Ed. Edwin Honig and Oscar Williams. New York: Washington Square Press, 1968.

Edinger, Edward F. *Anatomy of the Psyche.* La Salle, Ill.: Open Court, 1985.

———. *The Bible and the Psyche: Individuation Symbolism in the Old Testament.* Toronto: Inner City Books, 1986.

———. *The Creation of Consciousness: Jung's Myth for Modern Man.* Toronto: Inner City Books, 1984.

———. *Ego and Archetype: Individuation and the Religious Function of the Psyche.* New York: Putnams, 1972.

Frazer, James G. *The Golden Bough.* 3rd ed. 13 vols. London: Macmillan, 1919.

Guignebert, Charles. *Jesus.* New Hyde Park, N.Y.: University Books, 1966.

Hall, James. *Dictionary of Subjects and Symbols in Art.* New York: Harper and Row, 1974.

Harding, M. Esther. *Woman's Mysteries, Ancient and Modern.* New York: Pantheon Books, 1955.

Harrison, Jane. *Prolegomena to the Study of Greek Religion.* Cambridge: Cambridge University Press, 1922.

Hennecke, Edgar. *New Testament Apocrypha.* 2 vols. Ed. Wilhelm Schneemelcher. Philadelphia: The Westminster Press, 1963.

Hölderlin, Friedrich. *Poems and Fragments.* Trans. Michael Hamburger. Ann Arbor: University of Michigan Press, 1967.

Jerusalem Bible. Garden City, N.Y.: Doubleday and Co., 1966.

Jonas, Hans. *The Gnostic Religion*. Boston: Beacon Press, 1958.

Jung, C.G. *The Collected Works* (Bollingen Series XX). 20 vols. Trans. R.F.C. Hull. Ed. H. Read, M. Fordham, G. Adler, Wm. McGuire. Princeton: Princeton University Press, 1953-1979.

————. *C.G. Jung Speaking* (Bollingen Series XCVII). Ed. Wm. McGuire and R.F.C. Hull. Princeton: Princeton University Press, 1977.

————. *Memories, Dreams, Reflections*. Ed. Aniela Jaffé. Trans. Richard and Clara Winston. New York: Pantheon Books, 1963.

————. *Seminar 1925*. Mimeographed Notes of Seminar, March 23–July 6, 1925, Zurich.

Kazantzakis, Nikos. *The Saviors of God*. New York: Simon and Schuster, 1969.

Liddel and Scott. *Greek-English Lexicon*. Oxford: Oxford University Press, 1963.

The Mysteries: Papers from the Eranos Yearbooks. Vol. 2. New York: Pantheon Books, 1955.

Neumann, Erich. *Depth Psychology and a New Ethic*. Trans. Eugene Rolfe. New York: Putnams, 1969.

Origen on First Principles. Trans. G.W. Butterworth. New York: Harper Torchbooks, Harper and Row, 1966.

Patai, Raphael. *The Messiah Texts*. New York: Avon Books, 1979.

Pistis Sophia. Trans. G.R.S. Mead. London: John M. Watkins, 1947.

Shakespeare, William. *The Complete Works*. London: Oxford University Press, 1965.

Smith, George D., ed. *The Teaching of the Catholic Church*. 2 vols. New York: Macmillan, 1964.

Vine, W.E. *An Expository Dictionary of New Testament Words*. Old Tappan, N.J.: Fleming H. Revell Co., 1966.

Voragine, Jacobus de. *The Golden Legend*. Trans. Granger Ryan and Helmut Ripperger. New York: Longmans, Green and Co., 1948.

Index

Numbers in italics refer to illustrations